LIFE WITHOUT LIMITS

Discover the Secrets to Your
Personal Empowerment
and a Life of Ecstatic Joy

By Peter Calhoun with Astrid Ganz

Cover Photo Credit: "Star Forming Region LH 95 in the Large Magellanic Cloud" by NASA, ESA and The Hubble Heritage Team

Cover Layout and Design: Tamara Albright, Albright Creative

CLAIM EXCLUSIVE
BONUS CONTENT
available only at
LifeWithoutLimitsBook.com

To further connect with Peter and Astrid, please go to http://LifeWithoutLimitsBook.com to receive additional bonus content that will only be made available there, including a teleseminar in which Peter reveals more of his life story, and discusses how you can put the lessons contained within *Life Without Limits* to work in your own life.

Whether you simply want to develop your own personal practice, or would like direct mentoring with Peter through his shamanic training workshops, vision quests, or apprenticeship programs, go to LifeWithoutLimitsBook.com to learn more and to connect with others on the path.

Peter is also available on a limited basis for personal readings and healing sessions. You may contact him at info@petercalhoun.com.

WHAT PEOPLE ARE SAYING ABOUT PETER

"Thank you for your superb presentation at our 2008 National Coptic Conference in Olivet, Michigan. Based on numerous responses from the audience in attendance, your presentation received a phenomenal positive response."

John Davis, Director of Coptic Fellowship International & the Spiritual Unity of Nations, Author of *Messiah & the Second Coming* (1981) & *Revelation for Our Time* (1997)

"The book signing featuring Peter Calhoun and his book *Soul on Fire* was one of our most successful ever. The store overflowed with a standing-room-only group of eager participants who were inspired and uplifted by his message, and who purchased many books!"

Emory Michael, Owner of Luminata Books, Monterey, CA

"We were fortunate enough to have Peter Calhoun speak at our Sunday morning service this past October (2007), and his was one of our best-attended services. He drew a large percentage of our members and many visitors, more than any other special speaker in our recent history."

Joseph W. Miller, Member of the Worship Committee of Westside   **Unitarian Universalist Church, Knoxville, TN**

"We had a phenomenal weekend with Peter and Astrid! We sold the most books any author event has had…. Astrid and Peter are a phenomenal team. Peter, at age 72, has so much wisdom and so much to teach. He is a great teacher. His teachings are almost St. Francis-like … so pure, so true, so simple. His teachings are what we need to hear today."

Julie, founding director of Peace of Mind Emporium, Vermont

"When I saw you speak at the seminar before several hundred people, I began to sob uncontrollably. I felt as though you were speaking to and from my heart and my soul. I know a good deal about the various religious paths of the world. That's my job as an Interfaith Minister – and I've tried many of these paths … But, then, I heard you speak, and no book (and I've read lots) or path, or person, has resonated with me as you did. The woman next to me during the seminar whispered, 'Welcome home!' How did she know?"

Rev. G. D.

"Warmest thanks for the remarkable treasure of your visit to mark our 48th church anniversary. You are such a remarkable teacher, Peter. You've become a spiritual elder, storyteller, and true visionary. Every comment I've heard has been positive, exceptional, deeply affirmative of the content and quality of your presentation. [Astrid is] a radiant, eloquent, powerful, spirited being. How blessed you (both) are …"

**Rev. LeRoy Zempke, Pastor of the Temple of the Living God,
St. Petersburg**

ACKNOWLEDGMENTS

Peter and Astrid wish to express their deepest gratitude to Carol Kahn, Marjorie Hilliard, Rev. Glenda Dannenfelser and Susan Blue for their generous time, editorial skills, creativity and inspiration, whose expertise and dedication to our cause meant far more to us than words can express.

We also wish to express our deepest thanks to Renee Harrington and Ron Brassfield for their generous time, expertise and support – and to Mary Byrd whose great generosity, thoughtfulness and compassion enabled us to take the next step in our lives.

Our deepest gratitude to Pam Lambert and Mike Mickley, without whose great generosity, editorial skills, sage advice, continual support on every level and belief in our vision of what could be, this book could not have been birthed.

Each of these persons truly walks their talk. Thank you many times over.

Table of Contents

A Message from Astrid

As some of you already know, it has been Peter's desire to have an account for the Western world of the awakening of his *siddhis*. He hopes that this could be a guide for others who might be going through similar experiences. In the pages that follow he has given this account.

As one who knows Peter better than anyone else, it is appropriate for me to describe some of the things I have witnessed since we met in November of 1996. Often I have joined him in these events as my own abilities have begun to unfold.

And yet before proceeding further, I would have to ask: **"How does one speak about that for which there are no words?"** The manifestation of the *siddhis* is among the highest expressions of the soul.

Few in the West have any idea of how remarkable it is for someone in our culture to experience a full awakening of their soul powers. Our society does not recognize such an accomplishment or even acknowledge that these powers exist. One rarely hears of anyone in our culture who has repeatedly demonstrated these abilities as Peter has done on many occasions.

Peter has often said that his path would have been vastly easier if he had grown up in India, Tibet or almost any of the Eastern cultures. It is also true that if he had had a teacher it would have been far easier, but that was not his destiny. From what we know of the lives of the great masters, most of them had extremely talented and wise mentors to help awaken their own powers while they were still quite young.

In *Life Without Limits* Peter vividly describes the awakening of an ability to spontaneously combust ceremonial fires, to self-combust, and to call in the Fire element for a variety of purposes. He also writes about his survival of a full lightning strike with no apparent harm. In addition, he shares stories of his materialization of storms, his control of thunder and lightning, and times he was able to call up or stop the wind. As many of you know these feats are part of the

Command over the Elements that has been a part of *cross-cultural shamanism* as well as in many Eastern traditions.

His stories of teleportation and bilocation as well as his intervention using sacred ceremonies for a friend or family member soon to be facing a life-threatening situation, are further demonstrations of the awakening of his soul powers.

In his first book, *Soul on Fire,* Peter describes his experience of being accepted into a herd of bighorn sheep and also with a family of deer. Ecstatic relationship with many species of animals and birds is one of the great joys we both have shared. During the last decade, together or separately, we have been able to call to us nearly two dozen species of animals and birds including a herd of bison, deer, elk, bears, coyotes, cougars, bobcats, foxes, black snakes, hawks and eagles, and even a tiny praying mantis. Although each one of these animal encounters has its own peculiar *energetic signature,* I still believe that our calling the century-long extinct panther back to the Smoky Mountains was our crowning achievement.

Another very unusual *siddhi* Peter writes about is his remarkable protection on at least seven different occasions against imminent and almost certain death, at least one of which was a deliberate attempt on his life. When asked the obvious question: "How is it that someone could have so many different kinds of life-threatening situations arise?" Peter just laughs saying, "Few people have any concept of what a high-risk calling this Path can be."

The awakening of Peter's *shakti,* like that of teleportation, is another example of what has been called the "high *siddhis.*" As early as the late 80s Peter discovered that some people experienced spontaneous healing while talking to him over the phone or the moment he walked into a hospital room. Like that which has been attributed to some of the Eastern masters, Peter's *shakti* is transmitted through both voice and eye contact as well as by his presence. On one occasion Peter's presence precipitated a spontaneous spiritual transformation in a drug dealer even though the person was not seeking to change his life.

Several more of the *siddhis* that have awakened in Peter are worth mentioning. Peter was able to use his intention to heal four dying hemlocks on our property. The trees had been stricken by a blight that had already killed more than half the species in the Smoky Mountain National Park. On four different occasions we were able to totally clear the pollution out of our area for a period of ten to fourteen days and a radius of twenty to thirty miles. It might be worth mentioning that the Smoky Mountain National Park, which is only a few miles from our former home in eastern Tennessee, is the most polluted park in the country.

One of the *siddhis* Peter does not fully describe is the spontaneous awakening of the ability to dream musical scores and then to consciously hear the music. I have heard some of the music performed and recorded on cassette tape and will have to say that his Renaissance type of music is quite beautiful.

Does Peter believe every moment of the day that he is without limits? When Peter first received his vision of the limitlessness of who we all are, he was functioning on a very high level of awareness. Neither of us is always on that level. On several occasions in spite of his miraculous experiences, I have seen him struggle with doubt and uncertainty. In such cases, like any loving partner, I encouraged him, reminding him of his many accomplishments. During those times I have said to Peter: "With your intention, you can do anything you choose to do! You have proved that time and again!" In some ways it seems incredible to me that Peter could have any doubts at all. Few people in the West have any idea how all-inclusive an awakening of these soul powers can be.

But anyone can claim anything and some have, but without being able to back up those claims. By contrast nearly all of the stories that appear in Peter's writings were witnessed by two or more people, sometimes by as many as several dozen. I would add that Peter has never claimed to have special powers, always insisting that these abilities are in all of us.

To assist the seriously committed students to begin awakening their own powers, we developed a teaching technique which produces results that are immediate, impressive and undeniable. These awakenings are understood to be a natural flowering of consciousness when the time is ripe. In fact to attempt to block or disregard this flowering as some have been told to do by their teachers would seem to be unnatural and a denial of the natural unfoldment of consciousness.

Our greatest desire is that all of you who read of his demonstrations will not attempt to place Peter on a pedestal. Instead Peter wishes to be known simply as one who has remembered who he is and who we all are. In this great new cycle we are now poised to enter, a growing number of people are beginning to awaken their own spiritual powers that have long been dormant in the vast majority of our species.

Of the spontaneous awakening of his soul powers, Peter states: "I was experiencing a whole new way of being. It was like waking up for the first time and realizing who I truly was. In fact, it is who all of us are."

Peter likens most people to the pilot who is flying through a raging storm and is getting beaten up and tossed around. Someone tells him that he can fly above the storm, but he does not believe it is possible and besides he is into the struggle, the pain and the fear. A part of him believes that if he gives up all of this, then he will no longer be himself. What one loses, of course, is ego in all of its many subtle and veiled manifestations.

One of the things that impressed me about Peter from the beginning was his deep appreciation for women and the Divine Feminine. He has always regarded and treated me as an equal in every respect. In *Soul on Fire* he writes about several of his visitations by the Greek Goddess, Artemis, who called him a "servant of the goddess who will bring many people back to the Earth Mother." Artemis Huntress is the protectress of women, children and animals as well as the Goddess of Nature Magic of which Peter is so adept. In addition he has experienced several direct encounters with Gaia herself.

Because this work can get quite intense, there are times I have had to help Peter lighten up. Peter knows he can sometimes get too heavy and overly serious and greatly appreciates what he calls my "gift for holy laughter," pointing out that this too is considered one of the high *siddhis*. Sometimes my role is to point out the humorous spin-offs that can occur totally unexpectedly in our work. One of my favorite stories was about a comment made by Todd, a very bright young man a few years out of college, who was assisting with the editing of *Soul on Fire*. During the months of his editing Peter's manuscript, I found him intrigued by the stories of Peter's experiences. Something however was bothering him but neither Peter nor I had any idea what.

Finally when the manuscript was completed, Todd hesitantly asked the question that we realized had been haunting him all along: "When you were having all of those experiences you were writing about, what were you using?"

Peter hesitated for a moment, uncertain what Todd was getting at. Then it hit him. For the entire time of his editing *Soul on Fire*, Todd had assumed that Peter was using some kind of hallucinogenic drug, and I suspected that he was obsessed with the idea of trying it out for himself.

When Peter assured Todd that no drugs were involved and that it was the spiritual practices that precipitated these paranormal occurrences, he seemed shocked. It had not occurred to Todd that such things were possible without the use of drugs.
For weeks afterward whenever this story would come to our minds, we would practically double up with laughter.

"I don't want to be viewed as an example of how one should live," Peter said, "but for those who know me, it is obvious that I am no saint – in fact, far from it. Besides there is a **very** big difference between a saint and an enlightened person and one should not confuse the two. Most saints are far from being enlightened! Saint Francis and a few others are notable exceptions. And most enlightened persons definitely are not saints!"

One of Peter's former apprentices, perhaps best expressed the experience of studying with Peter: "Magic just seemed to follow you wherever you went. We all felt it was such a privilege to be allowed into your world." Many persons like that apprentice have found that same magic to awaken in them by just being in Peter's presence.

There are ancient records that speak of a time when the Earth was still young, that the Angelic Host created a species of human that was so perfect that there was nowhere to go. There was nothing to do because of the perfection of their creation. Realizing this, they had to discontinue that species and start all over again. The result is the human that is us. The Angelic Host realized that this time they got it right. *The perfection of this new creation was in its imperfection* and yet the spark of perfection was to be found deep within the essence of this new being that is us. They knew the time would come in the far distant future that the seed of perfection would be discovered and realized. That time is now.

The *siddhis* that awakened in Peter span such a wide diversity that if he tried to document all of them here, it would far exceed the space available. I hope I have given you an accurate profile of the person Peter really is. I have intended to give you a sampling of what qualifies him to pass along to you the wisdom and vision gained as a result of his experiences of awakening.

Foreword

An African shaman who has written several excellent books about his experience and training writes that each person comes into this Earth with a specific task that no one else can perform. The problem is we all forget what that task was.

I like what I feel about this person because I know he also has had many experiences of this magical world we live in.

When I came into this life as a "walk-in," having died during the Holocaust and swapping places with a six-year-old boy walking home from school who very much wanted out, I kept repeating over and over again, as if it were my mantra for this incarnation, "I've got to remember who I am."

In some ways, I recognized the above was the key to my soul purpose, but of course, like everyone else, I promptly forgot.

In 1970, while serving as a priest in the Episcopal Church, I had the good fortune to be shown my life's purpose in an epic vision. It turned my world upside-down! In the vision, I was told that my task was to remember all that I had been, to awaken the spiritual powers I had developed in other lifetimes, and be able to demonstrate these as abilities latent in all of us.

I was also told that I would have no teacher in this lifetime, but part of my demonstration would be to show that we all have this ability to accomplish these things on our own, because in this New Cycle that was being ushered in, there would be millions awakening, and not nearly enough teachers to assist this number.

Looking back over my life, I still wonder, "Why me?" There must be a number of others who could have done a better job. And yet, in the end, after much struggle, I feel that I finally was able to achieve my soul's purpose for this lifetime.

This book, therefore, is my offering to all of you who are ready to break through the limitations of our consensus reality culture and, as you were intended by our wondrous Creator, to soar like the eagles
.

Prologue: The Ripple Effect

A pebble dropped into a body of water creates ripples that move out in ever-widening concentric circles, reaching shores undreamed of and touching lives far beyond our awareness. What is touched then responds by setting off new ripples, which in turn create still more ripples. The above has been called "The Ripple Effect."

Whenever you have the courage to speak your truth, to expose the lies – the deliberate deception – as well as the rampant ignorance in our world, then you have become a spokesperson for that Truth that has no opposite.

When finally you are able to give a demonstration for the Truth that we are beings who are not limited by the laws of the physical plane, then no longer are you just a spokesperson but a doer – a demonstrator of Truth.

Finally, when you have transcended the laws of the physical plane by demonstrating again and again the limitlessness of who we all are, then you have achieved the highest level, which is to become a living embodiment of the same Truth that will liberate our humanity from its prison without walls.

The stone that I now throw into the deep pool of our collective human consciousness is the idea of the limitlessness of that which you are as individualized manifestations of an Infinite Creator.

The ripples that are produced by this stone are the text of this book, which in stories and metaphor, speaks deep truths about your true nature as a magical and infinite being living in a magical world.

As these ripples touch you and many others, a few of you will "get it" and break free of your prisons without walls, pushing for the first time through the web of deception and illusion, that ceiling of false beliefs that are so limiting, suppressive and disempowering, which are the source of so much suffering in our world.

In this way, you, in turn, create new ripples that touch the lives of a few others, who will also "get it," knowing for the first time that Truth that sets all beings forever free. And they, in turn, will send out further ripples, until a critical mass is reached that will change the DNA of our species, which will be forever transformed without most even realizing what has happened.

Namaste,
Peter (Snow Eagle)

Chapter 1: Claiming a Great Promise

A Ceiling over the Earth

When I was still a priest in the Episcopal Church, I had an out-of-body experience in which I saw the Earth from perhaps one-third of the way to the moon. I saw something that covered the Earth. It seemed artificial and out of place, as if it did not belong. Whatever it was, it did not feel good to me. It was a kind of ceiling that had been placed there, which appeared to prevent the people on Earth from being able to grow. I perceived that most of the people on Earth were stooped over like hunchbacks because they had been unable to break through the ceiling. I was told that because of this ceiling most people on Earth are unable to get beyond the emotional level of spiritual adolescence. I was told by the cathedral voice that always accompanies my visions that this ceiling had been constructed over a period of many centuries by a spiritual, economic and political elite, and that this elite consisted of a number of the power brokers of our world. They did not understand compassion. They did not understand the first principle of free will. They understood one thing and one thing only – power over and control of other people. I was told that this had become a veritable prison camp, and that the people on Earth had no awareness of this prison because it was a prison without walls – a prison of false beliefs imposed on the people of Earth, and this false belief system had become part of the consensus reality of the major cultures of the world. This consensus reality made up of these false belief systems was reinforced daily by the controlled media and supported by the religious, political, economic and even the scientific institutions to a certain extent.

I was told that although there were power brokers who had the best interests of the world at heart, this particular group of elitists constituted a very dark and secret cabal who worked to gain control of the money, the power and the knowledge, keeping everyone else good "worker bees" to serve the needs of the elite.

The Family of Light

After a long pause enabling this idea to be assimilated, the voice continued, explaining that I was part of a large grouping of souls that had come here from many parts of the universe to throw off this ceiling and liberate the people of this beloved Earth. We were known by many names, but the voice speaking to me chose to refer to us as the Family of Light. Most of you reading these words are a part of this family, and that is why you resonate with them. We were to do this by incarnating, and we would instinctively know how to break through this ceiling. In demonstrating how we do this, others would understand how to break through and liberate the planet Earth. I was told most of us had incarnated here many times, and that with this family of souls we had a special talent. We could come into any world and instinctively break through any suppressive system and recognize the falsity of it. We were, in fact, revered throughout the universe for this ability and for our courage.

The voice told me that even though we had accomplished this in other worlds many times in the past, this would be our most difficult assignment, so powerful were the "controllers" and so effective was their almost impenetrable ceiling. I was told that we had come into incarnation in many parts of the world. Our task would be to keep a low profile at first and gather information. We would need to understand how the cabal operates and how their "ceiling" works.

I was told that I would need to keep a lower profile at that time, as I had been appearing on numerous television and radio talk shows, because too much visibility from speaking out against the system or demonstrating spiritual powers would cause me to be recognized as a member of that Family of Light.

The above, in fact, was one of the ways the controllers remained in power – by singling out those who were easily breaking through the ceiling, and eliminating them. I was then shown the faces of John and Robert Kennedy, Martin Luther King, Jr., and other international figures as examples of our Family members that had been eliminated as a result of their high profiles.

The voice then told me we would first have to link up. This would be an automatic thing that would happen when we encountered other Family members. We would recognize one another by "a vibration in the tip of the sternum," which I interpreted to mean a heart feeling.

From that time on, even if we were on opposite sides of the globe, we would be connected by an energetic band of light.

As the "linking up" progressed, we would become connected to millions of other Family members as the result of a worldwide grid of light that had been formed. Once this had happened, we would not be so vulnerable because this grid of light would give us great protection, and when we acted, we would act with the power of the whole.

I was told that this false belief system that had been imposed on us was limiting, suppressive and disempowering to the people of Earth. It was enforced almost daily by a controlled media and supported to a great extent by the economic, political, military, educational, medical and even scientific institutions. Finally, I was told that this false belief system was directly or indirectly the source of most of the suffering in our world.

This epic vision was the first of a series of visions about the status of our world and its probable future. One can well imagine how I as a priest of a mainstream church was affected. My world was turned upside down. After this epic vision, which lasted most of the night (and it was my first vision, actually), I recalled a dream that had recurred throughout my life of being in a concentration camp. Always the dream would leave me with an enormous frustration, depression and feeling of being trapped. Then one day I had this same dream again, and I noticed that one whole wall was missing in the prison camp. It had consisted of twenty-foot tall barbed wire fences with guard towers every twenty feet. I was totally shocked that all this time one whole wall had been missing. I looked out over a beautiful prairie with multicolored flowers, and in the distance I saw beautiful, snow-capped mountains. I thought, all this time I could simply have walked out, but I never knew it: I was staying of my own volition. In this dream, I chose to just walk out. There was some fear of being killed by machine guns in the guard towers, but nothing happened, and soon I was walking through the beautiful prairie toward the snow-capped mountains and freedom. Once I had had this dream of actually walking out of the concentration camp, it never occurred again and I realized I was being shown the state of affairs on Earth. Earth was a prison camp, but the incredible secret is that none of us are here against our will. All of us are free to simply walk out by recognizing the false belief systems that we have accepted since our parents and other adults first imposed upon us their version of the world. And, of course, we bought into this. It was not their fault because they had been taught the same thing by their own parents, pastors, rabbis, family members and teachers since they were toddlers and school children.

My Life Purpose Revealed

It was during this period that I had another out-of-body experience, during which I saw this book suspended in light. The book was open about halfway and I saw that my name was on it. To my surprise, the cathedral voice told me that this was a book I would someday write. The voice began reading from the book, and it was a book of stories about my spiritual journey and experiences while I was on this journey. At that time, since I was still a priest in the church, the experiences seemed both incredible and unattainable. I was then told about my purpose for coming to Earth at this time in Earth's history.

I was shown that in this lifetime I would have no teacher, which came as a huge disappointment to me. For years I had had a great desire to bask in the aura of a great teacher or guru. I was told I had incarnated into this Earth with total loss of memory of who I was, and it was my task to remember all that I had been and reawaken abilities from other lifetimes. I was not only to awaken them but to demonstrate them as abilities that are latent within all of us. I was to demonstrate that we can awaken these abilities through our direct relationship with the Creator, as opposed to that of a mystery school, guru or great teacher. This in fact would be the path of most human beings in the New Cycle. We would realize that we all have the ability to remember who we are and to awaken our abilities though a direct relationship with the Creator. Thus, I was given the spiritual mandate to remember, then awaken, and then demonstrate. It would be through my demonstration that people could understand that we each have the ability to have a direct connection with our Creator without requiring a teacher. I also was told that I had achieved "liberation" in a previous lifetime, but that I had deliberately chosen to forget who I was at this time of incarnating. Otherwise my demonstration would be meaningless. This revelation helped me to understand the words I kept repeating when I came into this life as a "walk-in." For the words I was repeating over and over again, as I was preparing to merge with the body of a six-year old boy walking home from the first grade on Peachtree Street in Atlanta, were spoken with a sense of urgency, almost as if it were a mantra: "I've got to remember who I am! I've got to remember who I am!" At first I interpreted that to mean, remember my last life in which I died in the Holocaust. In time I realized that I was affirming my soul purpose for this life: "to fully and completely remember who I am as a spiritual being."

The young boy whose place I took very much wanted out, as he realized that he was not prepared for another life on Earth. I, on the other hand, wanted to begin my new life on Earth and bypass the usual method of experiencing childbirth. It is a way that a soul can reverse its decision to begin another Earth life without any karmic debt. It is also a way in which a more advanced soul can bypass the usual procedure of childbirth and even in some cases the process of growing up.

This task of remembering and demonstrating abilities from past lives seemed grandiose and impossible, and yet it happened over a period of three decades with an amazing spontaneity and effortlessness, as if preordained and orchestrated from some higher realm.

The Great Promise of Christ

But then I felt there was no way that I could possibly awaken abilities that I may have developed in other lifetimes that I could not even remember. After I was shown the vision of the book, I pondered this for many days afterwards. What was I to do? How was I to do it?

One day I realized that, since I had been ordained as a priest in the church, and even before that, I had been haunted by a certain passage of scripture: "Why are ye so amazed? These things and more shall you be able to do." These, of course, were the words of Jesus of Nazareth to his followers. I wondered why so few throughout history had claimed this promise. Saint Francis did, but why were there not a hundred or even a thousand Saint Francises around at any given time? When I talked with some of my colleagues in the clergy about this, they felt it was not meant that everyone would have these abilities. They said Jesus was either speaking metaphorically or it was for the disciples only. I began to realize that so many of us in my own religious affiliation had a selective belief when it came to the Scripture. We believed in what made us comfortable, but we discounted that which is troublesome or confusing.

Being Put to the Test

I made the decision to lay claim to this promise, or at least to prove or disprove its validity. It was only two weeks later that I was put to the test. I was called to a downtown hospital in Atlanta to see a woman I had never met but claimed Episcopal affiliation. I found out from the nurse supervisor that she had been given the medical sentence of death. She had cancer, which had spread throughout her body, and was expected to live no more than another forty-eight hours. While I was visiting with her and speaking with her, I asked if she desired healing and she said she did. So I gave her healing, wondering the whole time if I was doing it right or just raising her hopes for nothing, setting her up for disappointment. Was I egotistical to think I could actually help her? I felt nothing. Meanwhile, in the weeks and months that followed, I assumed she had passed away as predicted. It was six months later that I heard there was a woman going around Atlanta telling everyone about the priest that had healed her. It was the same woman. Of course, I wondered why she never bothered to tell me, but perhaps she thought I would just know. I pondered what had happened for many days afterward.

Awakening of Shakti

The above story and the three that follow appear at the beginning of Last Hope on Earth, the book on healing co-authored by Astrid and me. However, I felt that they should be included here, since they were a large part of the process of my awakening.

Then it seemed almost as if one thing after another happened and that I was on a fast track in spiritual awakening. It seemed also that a part of me was acting out a script that had already been written.

One of the things that happened very quickly was discovery of a type of power called shakti. I did not know at the time, but learned later, that shakti in Vedic teachings is considered the Primal Feminine Force of Creation. Many of the Eastern masters are supposed to have strong shakti that they can transfer to their students.

One of my first experiences with shakti was with a man who called me from California. He had met a woman from Aspen I had worked with, and, according to her, had saved her from dying of arsenic poisoning. She had told him about me and he wanted to know if he could fly to Atlanta so I could work with him. As we were going over our calendars to set up a date for him to fly, I felt a force go out from my heart and solar plexus. I did not know what it was, so I just decided to stop talking. After a few minutes he said he was feeling very strange. I knew he had received the shakti I had just experienced. I told him I thought we had just saved him the cost of a plane ticket. We had! He was healed by the shakti that had gone out from me: somehow it touched and transformed the life of this man I had never met, who seemingly had no spiritual or religious inclinations, and with whom I felt no real connection.

I was reminded by this of certain healing episodes in the New Testament. One that came to mind was the woman who touched the hem of Christ's garment when he was speaking to the masses. He asked who touched him. His disciples told him many were touching him because he was surrounded by them, but he said that no, he felt this power go out from him. I believe this was the same thing I was experiencing.

The Most Wonderful Feeling Ever

The next time this happened, I had traveled three hours to visit a woman in the hospital who had cancer. I had questioned why I had made this long drive. I did not feel I could help her and I was exhausted. I had a lot of things happening in my life that were very stressful. When I walked into the hospital room, I saw it filled with long-faced family members. As soon as my eyes met the woman's in the bed, I felt a power come out through me. She asked what was going on, because she was feeling hot all over. She said it was the most wonderful feeling she had ever had in her life. One of the family members asked who had turned the heat up. They felt the temperature had gone up about ten degrees, and they had to leave. It was the fastest I have ever seen a hospital room empty.

My "Last Hope on Earth"

Another episode that comes to mind is with a woman who had been a spiritual leader and was a psychotherapist in her community. This in fact provided the inspiration for the title of our book, Last Hope on Earth. This particular woman had, for unknown reasons, suddenly gone into a psychological and physical disintegration. She ended up in bed in the fetal position for about six months. A number of healers, including some Lakota Sioux shamans, had tried unsuccessfully to work with her. One of the Lakota shamans told her he was not working with her anymore, because bad things were happening to everyone who tried to work with her. She wanted to see if I could work with her, but I was hesitant. I had heard of this kind of thing before and did not know that I would be able to protect my family, much less myself. In fact, I at first refused to work with her, but was told she had stated that I was her "last hope on Earth." How does one refuse something like that? So I agreed to meet with her. She and I set a date for her to fly to Atlanta. We had a long talk and she asked question after question. Then she called twice more in the next two weeks. Each time we spoke for about forty-five minutes. I should have realized that something was happening but it did not occur to me. Finally she called a third time and told me she no longer needed to see me. She said, "I am healed. Your shakti healed me." That was why she kept calling, because she could feel the shakti coming through my voice, which according to her was responsible for her healing.

Remembering My Past Lives

It was during this time that I began to spontaneously recall past lives. I was told that I had to do this, and yet it seemed to happen effortlessly along with my spiritual practices, just as my soul powers, the *siddhis*, were awakened spo
ntaneously.

Following Buddha's Teachings about Remembering

Buddha taught that it was necessary to recall all of our past lives to attain enlightenment. Other teachers, however, are silent about this, so there may not be universal agreement among the masters. Buddha recalled all of his lives simultaneously. For me, it was a situation of recalling them as needed. The memory of a past life would illuminate the meaning of a challenge in this life. In this way, over a period of several decades I remembered more than a hundred lifetimes.

Healing My Past

I not only remembered these lifetimes, but I had to also understand the lesson of each. Buddha pointed out the need to know the lesson of each lifetime. I discovered that, as far as the lesson learned from it, an entire lifetime could be summed up in a single line. For example, there was one life when I was a sea captain who was an alcoholic. I thought that surely was a wasted life. But I was told that was one of my most important lifetimes because I learned the meaning of waste and would never again waste the opportunity of being in this world.

Not only did I have to recall past lives and to know the lesson of each life, but I had to release any residual emotions. So where there was pain, anger or fear, this had to be released. For example in my most recent Native American lifetime as a Lakota Sioux, there was enormous pain. I not only lost loved ones, but I lost a whole way of life that I had cherished. It was a life with one big extended family which was the tribe, and a life in which we were able to live in total harmony with the Earth and all Nature. I longed to experience that life again, with the extended family of the tribe, and to experience that absolute harmony with physical Creation. I was told that this would hold me back and that these unresolved emotions had to be released. I was told that it was not just so-called negative emotions that hold us back, but we have to release the positive ones also. For instance, a life in which one experienced perfect love could give rise to a longing to repeat that life, so I would need to release it because it creates dissatisfaction with the present.

Canceling "Groundhog Day"

As it turned out, I was not only able to recall my past lifetimes here on Earth but was able to spontaneously access the past lives of others when there was a need for that person to know. Again and again, I could see people's blockages often originate before their present life here on Earth.

There is something else that was very important about this, having to do with something Buddha observed. He saw that the greatest problem for human beings was not the karma they had created, but it was the "cycle of recurrence." He talked about the tendency of humans to make the same bad choices, choose the same bad relationships, and make the same kinds of mistakes because there was a type of negative magnetism. We could be drawn back to having a relationship with a murderer or rapist in another lifetime, because we would feel the magnetism but not necessarily interpret it as negative. We could be tempted to repeat another life as a soldier or a monk, perhaps, because we experienced the magnetism even though it could have been a disastrous life. This is the cycle of recurrence. The way I put it is that we have to cancel Groundhog Day. I refer, of course, to the movie in which the well-known actor, Bill Murray, found himself waking up each morning only to live out the same life over again each day, and being always able to anticipate what would happen next. This is the nature of life on the physical plane. It seems we are simply repeating the same thing over and over again much of the time without realizing that we are. We seldom are able to break free of this endless cycle of recurrence that Buddha so astutely observed.

One unusual aspect of my ability to recall my past lives and those of others was that I was able to do this in a fully aware state. It is usually done by mediums in a deep trance state. This ability later proved invaluable beyond measure when my partner and I got involved in a very extensive healing practice.

Disempowerment from False Beliefs of the Times

What I discovered is that we have the illusion of making progress when in reality we are just recycling the same old experience over and over again. It is just that the cycles, which span lifetimes, are too great for us to become aware of the repetitive nature of our lives.

One of the false beliefs that has become deeply entrenched in our Western culture is the idea that we are here for the first time and have only one life to live. It has caused a lot of confusion about what life is all about.

Another false belief that has caused much of the suffering in this world is that we are limited beings. This is deeply entrenched in our religions and our culture. For example, all of us who grew up with a mainstream religion love hearing the stories of Jesus stilling the storm, Moses parting the sea, or Saint Francis communicating with animals and having wild animals come to him. Yet we were told that these abilities were present only in a few great souls living in the remote past and had nothing to do with us. I was told that the exact opposite was true. These great souls came to show us who we are and to help us remember these abilities. We all have these abilities or siddhis latent within us. In fact there was a time in remote antiquity in which many of us were able to demonstrate the soul powers. When we fell, we fell a long way, and for the most part we lost these abilities. This is part of the reawakening in this New Cycle that is upon us.

My First Animal Communication

As I began living out my vision, my connection with the natural world changed drastically. I learned, for example, that I could communicate with animals and that they were continually communicating with us through pictures and feelings, not through the rational mind. We just did not realize it.

I also sensed their frustration that we "two-leggeds" just did not get it. In their minds we were somewhat retarded. The first time this happened I was having dinner with a student. Her little Sheltie, Suzie, was all over me even while I was trying to eat. It was quite annoying. My host, Lori, had been looking at me with a wry, little smile. I asked what was behind her look. She was wondering what was so different about me, because her Sheltie had never had anything to do with men. I confessed to her that I did not know, but even as I was saying this, I realized that her animal companion was not just being annoying but was trying to communicate something to me. And then I knew. Suzie apparently had sensed I was able to understand.

The Sheltie told me she had been very depressed, which my host confirmed, although she did not know why. Suzie told me she had not been given any bones lately, and had not been taken for rides in the automobile, and that there was a big black dog nearby that she was afraid of. Lori was amazed. She said her dog loved bones, but she had been too busy teaching school to stop by the local meat market. She confirmed that Suzie's favorite thing to do was to ride in a car with her head hanging out the window, but they had not done that in a long time. Suzie also told me that now my student took her for walks on a route which brought them by a black Doberman. Although the Doberman was fenced in, it would lunge and growl menacingly. Lori could see her Sheltie shaking in fear when this happened. I told Lori she needed to use a different route for their walks, give Suzie bones, and take her for rides in the car. It seemed simple enough to me.

A few months later I was invited to dinner again. This time the Sheltie was very affectionate but extremely calm. Suzie said Lori had started giving her bones, taking her for rides, and had picked a different route for their walks. I realized that the little animal was expressing her thanks for my being her counselor and her advocate.

The Moses Effect

I learned a lot about the power of unconscious intention during the time I was doing a workshop at a palatial home on the bayou outside of New Orleans. We had begun talking about synchronicity and animal signs, and people got onto the synchronicity of serpents. Almost everyone had a story to tell. After a while I felt we were spending way too much time on this one subject and needed to move on because everyone seemed so obsessed with serpents. It was then that our hostess announced that we would break for lunch and should get our buffet lunch and take it out on the bayou to sit and eat. It was a beautiful day and seemed like a great idea. Once we all got out there, it took a few moments to comprehend what we saw. Curled up on every low overhanging limb, every log and on every rock was some sort of reptile. There must have been a hundred. We wondered if our hosts were playing a joke on us. There was no way we could eat out there. However, our hosts were just as shocked as we were. They had lived there for several years and had never seen the first snake. They did not even know of neighbors who had experienced anything like that. We called this the "Moses effect." But it became known as the "day of the serpents," because somehow the energies we were sending out in the stories we were telling had attracted this visitation. Somehow we had reached out to touch the group soul of the Great Serpent Spirit. We felt honored but cautiously kept our distance.

A "Command over the Elements"

Another thing that began to happen during this time was an unexpected development of a command over the Primal Forces of Creation. It was the last thing in the world I would dream of seeking. Yet I discovered that I had a type of relationship with the Fire, Water, Air and Earth elementals, and that I could influence these Primal Forces. In my study of cross cultural shamanism, I learned that this is a path that many shamans take. They seek to develop this command over the forces of Nature, because it is understood that command over the outer elements occurs only when one has command over the elements within. I discovered also that in the Vedic tradition this is a path that many of the Eastern masters take as well.

I learned that mastery or a command over these natural forces has nothing to do with "power over." This is our interpretation as a result of the patriarchal influence in our Western culture. It comes about almost through the opposite way. One must in fact learn to surrender to the Primal Forces. This is the real meaning of that often misunderstood expression.

Calling in the Storm of the Decade

I realized that the oneness I was achieving with the Creation around me had something to do with the awakening of these abilities. One of the first times I experienced this connection was in Northern Arizona, when I was visiting an area north of the community of Sedona called Oak Creek Canyon. I had learned they were in a two-and-a-half-year drought. The wells and streams were drying up and the area desperately needed water. This was in February of 1991. I was with a couple that had been apprenticing with me and I suggested we do a ceremony. The woman, whose name was Kathy, and I hiked over to a spring that flowed into Oak Creek. We felt this would be a good place to do our simple ceremony. The next morning I woke up and heard the sound of a limb breaking and then another limb breaking. I got up and looked out the window and there was a foot of snow on the ground. It turned out that northern Arizona had the storm of the decade at this time as well as the wettest spring on record.

Splitting a Storm in Half

I discovered I had a strong connection with the weather spirits. Since that time I have done over sixty ceremonies with about ninety-five percent success. I discovered that one could even influence these things at a distance. For example, one year my wife Astrid and I were getting ready to go to Canyonlands in Utah, where we had a group coming in for a vision quest. We learned from some friends in the area that there was a severe drought in that area, and according to reports, there was no water in the back country. About two weeks before we were to go there, I received the guidance that Astrid and I were to do a ceremony to bring rain. I wondered if this would work at a distance, because we were over three thousand miles away.

I did not need to worry because when we arrived two weeks later, we encountered a sight unusual for that high desert and canyon country in the Southwest. Every depressed area had standing water. It turned out that they'd had a monsoon, and it had rained for a week. We were told the rains were over and we were happy about that. There was now plenty of rain to give us water in the back country and to replenish the Earth as well. What a blessing this was! We were overjoyed that we had been able to influence this from a distance. On the fourth day of the vision quest, when the questers had loaded up their backpacks and were preparing to go on their solo period for three days and three nights, we saw a major storm coming in. The sky became black and there was continual lightning. We knew we were in for a terrific storm and did not know what to do, because they would not only get soaked but there could be some danger if the washes were to get flooded. We got the group together and asked the storm spirits to protect our vision questers and see that they stay dry. As one of our vision questers put it, "It was an amazing sight to see. It seemed that the storm just split in two and went around either side of us, and then came together when it got around us." We stayed high and dry. Not a drop of rain got on us and yet the Park Service had to close down an area adjacent to us when a ten-foot wall of water came down one of the major washes.

Mastery of the Fire Element

This command over the Primal Forces of Creation was one of the things that began to happen. In my book Soul on Fire, I talk about my first experience with spontaneous combustion, when sticks that had been laid for a ceremonial fire for our group of vision questers spontaneously combusted.

A second time, I had told another large group of seekers that I was setting my intention that we have another spontaneous combustion. We not only had spontaneous combustion in the pyramid of sticks that had been placed on the desert floor for a sweat lodge fire that was to be lit later that afternoon, but also in two other places where we had gathered kindling. This fire just appeared out of nowhere and was witnessed by most of our group. This was my first experience of realizing I had some command over the elemental force of Fire.

Clearing Pollution from the Skies through Intention

Years later I was given the guidance that one could use this same ability to command the elements to clear the pollution out of the skies. I tried this alone at the beginning of a particular summer. As I intended the pollution to lift, I also requested cobalt-blue "Western" skies with low humidity and mild temperatures in the 70s, in contrast to the usual high humidity with temperatures in the 90s. It seemed as if I had envisioned an impossible combination of elements for our area in the hot, humid South, yet that is exactly what I got. Forty-eight hours later the skies were crystal clear, totally free of pollution, and the humidity had dropped from eighty to twenty percent. The temperature at each midday averaged in the mid 70s. This was unheard of in our area because of the dense pollution occurring at that time of year from the heavy traffic going into the Smoky Mountains and the many coal-burning plants of Eastern Tennessee. The skies were a gem color and one could see something like crystals in the air. This appeared to extend for at least a twenty-mile radius. I was unable to learn if this unusual weather extended over the whole Park area. This phenomenon lasted a full two weeks. It was during this time that I had a chance to think about what I had accomplished and wondered if this could be repeated. I realized that if this were possible, there was almost no limit to what could be done to clean up pollution through intention. It is my intention to destroy this deeply entrenched belief that we are limited beings who are powerless to make a difference in our world.

Toward the end of the summer Astrid and I attempted the same feat. We had a group joining us for a week in August. We had rented a beautiful cottage in the Smokies. Astrid and I did a ceremony together and asked for pollution-free skies and dry, cool weather. We got just that and it lasted ten days. All this seemed to occur so fast that we hardly had time to assess what had happened, but we realized we had come into a new level of spiritual power that could help bring healing to our world. What were the possibilities or the limits to what we could do? As I write these words, Astrid and I have attempted this same feat several more times with the same dramatic results, with one exception when nothing happened. I have never been able to understand why sometimes all the intention and ceremonial work in the world seems to have no effect. This is rare, but it does occur.

Scientific Confirmation of the Enormous Power of Activating the "Light Body"

It was at this time that I learned of an internationally known teacher and shaman who had similar experiences of being able to clear the pollution. His results were equally dramatic, even though the pollution would immediately return when he stopped his meditative practices. But then it may not have been his intent to have a two-week reprieve as we did. He just wanted to see if it could be done. He also spoke about his conversation with an Air Force Colonel who informed him that a "satellite" had been picking up energies from the remote area where his group was staying. At first the Air Force personnel, monitoring him and other areas, thought that these were some new type of weapon because these energy sources were popping up more and more, not only in this country but around the planet. They finally realized that it was the "consciousness awakening happening around the planet." What she said was that "one person who has activated their light body puts out the same power as a city of 15,000." Because not all persons who have experienced this activation from spiritual practices are at the same level, I realized some persons may have considerably more power than that. This was the scientific support I had been looking for over the years. I knew that when one awakens their consciousness, the power one has is not measured in terms of mathematical increase. It is a quantum increase in power. It is vastly more powerful than that of the average person. This shows that, in the scientific sense of the word, we truly are able to transcend the laws of the physical plane. I think that on some deep core level, I have always known this.

I have come to realize that when one person performs a so-called miracle, that awakens something in others. Soon many people are bending the agreed-on limits of what is possible. I am told that only a very small number of people need to get the message that we are beings without limitation and that we can have this ecstatic relationship with the world around us. This is our birthright and entitlement. At a certain point then, we achieve critical mass and everyone gets it. It will be in the DNA of everyone, and they will accept that we all have the abilities to awaken these *siddhis* within ourselves.

Projection of the "Double" or Energetic Body

It was during this early period of development in the early and mid 70s that I began to experience something that was beyond the syntax of my culture and my philosophical and religious background. That was the ability to appear in other places in what seemed to be a physical presence or as a solid. This would happen in broad daylight at times where people could see me in physical form and could hear my voice. This was definitely not astral projection, which I had experienced many times and is far more common. The only frame of reference I had for this was later reading the Castaneda books, where much was written about the ability of certain Toltec shamans or sorcerers to project in what was called the "double" or "nahual," and to appear in a type of quasi-physical form. This happened before I even knew of the existence of the double.

The first time the above occurred was on a Sunday morning when I appeared to Israel, my dentist, in his living room. When he saw me he wondered, "What in the world is Peter doing in my living room on a Sunday morning?" He thought I had a lot of nerve, just walking into his living room unannounced.

Fire in the Basement

I told him to go down and check his basement. Something clicked inside and he knew something was wrong by the tone of my voice and the look of consternation on my face. He went down and saw that a fire had started from faulty wiring. He was able to call the fire department and get it put out in plenty of time. He came back up to thank me and I had disappeared. He realized that I must have been there in some other form. He called me the next morning to thank me for preventing his house from burning down.

An Unconventional Cure for Cocaine Addition

The next time this happened, I was lying awake in bed one evening when I was suddenly in the apartment of an apprentice whom I deeply loved. He was calling me with a sound of despair in his voice. I saw that he had just free-based cocaine and was feeling intense remorse. I had no idea he had a drug problem. But as I arrived unannounced at this apartment, I heard him saying, "Oh God help me, Jesus help me – Buddha, Peter please help me." Even in that unfamiliar state I could not help but catch the humor: I said to him that while I appreciated being put in that Pantheon of Deities; I was not really a part of that hierarchy, but I asked what I could do to help. I could see that he was in trouble. Even though he had just called me, when he saw me, he said, "Peter please, this is not the time. This is just not the time." I gave him some advice, and then I was back in my bed. The next morning I called him and repeated verbatim the conversation we had had the previous night and what had happened. As we were talking on the phone, I heard this thud. He had been so shocked he dropped the phone. He said he had convinced himself it was only a dream and could not believe I was actually physically present. As it turned out, my unannounced sudden appearance in his apartment that evening helped him kick his cocaine addiction.

A Surprise Teleportation

On another occasion I was with a group of apprentices in Grand Teton National Park. Our base camp was in the Gros Ventre Wilderness Area outside the National Park, so we could have fires and do a sweat lodge without having to deal with the bureaucratic rules of the Park Service. I was sitting on a log eating lunch with four or five other people. Suddenly I found myself half a mile away, looking at a steep trail that went up the side of a hill. I was concerned about what I was going to see and was scratching my head not knowing how I got there. Meanwhile the others were scratching their heads wondering what had happened to me. According to them, I had just vanished.

Then on the trail I saw one of our vision questers coming down the hill and immediately realized that she was ready to snap. That is why I was there. I do not know what got me there, but on some level I knew she was in desperate need of my help. This is a woman who, six months earlier, faced a crazed gunman who had broken into her house one Sunday morning with an arsenal of weapons. Then, holding her hostage at gunpoint, he threatened to blow up the house if she called the police. (As it turned out, he had already killed an entire family and a couple of policemen.) Soon her house was surrounded by SWAT teams, FBI agents, sheriffs and deputies. They had snipers set up around the house. All this was on national television. Eventually he blew up the house when he saw there was no way to keep from being apprehended. Her arm was nearly blown off. When I saw Mary, I threw my arms around her and she started shaking and making strange primal sounds. Soon she was sobbing and then screaming with terror. What I realized was that even though she had been with some of the best clinical psychologists in her area, the psychotherapy had been unable to touch the core pain. That core pain and terror, the enormous fear and anger, were coming out. I lifted her up and put her down on the ground in a fetal position and began rocking her. This is a very effective way to deal with someone who has gone into hysteria.

By this time there were several others who had joined to me. In fact a very interesting thing happened after I had rocked her for a while; two women gently tapped me on the shoulder and pushed me away. They wanted to have their turn. I thought I was doing a good job and was unsure why they felt they were supposed to be with her, but I acquiesced. They began rocking her, talking to her, and consoling her. Then it dawned on me that both of the women who had pushed me away and taken over had also had terrible abuse by men. They were the right people to be with her.

Controversy over the *Siddhis*

All of these miracles in my life greatly supported the information I had been given that we are beings without limitations. I have just shared several accounts of this experience of being in a quasi-physical body that had the ability to project anywhere. Unlike astral projection, there was a physical presence and my voice could be heard. It seemed everything was physical except the ability to instantly be in another place. This was part of my journey of discovery and these abilities, these *siddhis*, began to unfold spontaneously as a result of my spiritual practices. I want to make the point that in no way was I trying to develop these spiritual powers as ends in themselves. When they began to happen, I allowed rather than blocked them.

When we fell in Atlantis, we descended from a fifth dimensional culture to a mid-third dimensional culture. It is only in the third dimension that there is a total loss of memory of who we are. This is quite a fall. This loss of memory was a blessing. For us to remember what we had lost would have been unbearably painful. There is another reason we needed to have this descent: We had to make many changes, and it is only when we forget who we are that we are able to change. We can grow on every level, but only in the third dimension (third density) can we change. We lost these abilities, but they are soul powers that we once had. In this New Cycle, we will regain these powers. This is our destiny as human beings. Some will remember how to do these things, whether it is command over the elements, or projecting their double, or more common psychic abilities of telepathy, clairvoyance and healing. For me to have suppressed these because they could be ego-inflating or distractions on the path would have been like my parents telling me when I was learning to speak or walk that I should avoid these things as they could be ego-inflating or distractions. Can you imagine your parents saying this? My point is that these are just as much a part of our nature as human beings, part of our spiritual and physical nature, as learning to walk and learning to speak. Yes, there are some people who should stay away from these because they have demonstrated problems with the ego and are not ready to handle them, but there are many souls today ready for this awakening.

An Amazing Protection against Death

I became aware in retrospect that I had some kind of protection against death. This protection has allowed me to go on with my life when many times my life would have been cut short. My partner, Astrid, jokes about the fact that, like a cat, I have nine lives. I do not know how many I have used up. One of the stories in Soul on Fire was about the time that I was able to avoid flying on a doomed Continental flight from Denver to Boise. On take-off the plane flipped over because ice had formed on the wings. A number of people on the plane were killed. Because of a dream, which served as a warning to me, I was not on that flight.

Another time happened when I was vision questing alone in Utah. A voice came on a gentle breeze in the middle of the day and told me I must move my campsite, as it would be dangerous to be where I was. I had been sleeping under a massive cottonwood tree that was leaning at a thirty degree angle. It was very much alive and was four-to-five feet in diameter. It had seemed like a safe place to be. I reluctantly moved out into the open prairie. A gale force wind came in the night, and the only tree that went down was the one I had been sleeping under. When I walked back there, I was shocked that the trunk had snapped in two about ten feet up and had come down butt end first right where the imprint of my sleeping bag was. I would have been pulverized. Today my partner and I use this same magnificent area for our base camp with vision quest groups, a place that seems charged with the magical events of earlier years, including the four spontaneous combustions of ceremonial fires, and we love pointing out to them the huge fallen tree that should have ended my life.

Another near death experience was the time I hit black ice and fell thirty feet while traveling fifty miles per hour in my Toyota Forerunner, landing upside down and rolling. I did not have a seatbelt, and the people from 911 said there was no way anyone should have lived through that. I did not even have a bruise or a scratch. That seems to defy the laws of physics.

I have described the protection I have against fire at a time when I combusted during a fire ceremony, but was unharmed. Another amazing experience I had with the protection that comes from my command over the Fire element was the time I was struck by lightning while walking in a horse pasture during a thunderstorm. The horse that was walking with me was killed by a lightning bolt that hit it right after. It would have been bizarre to see from a distance: When the lightning struck, it went into me and through my left arm and left leg, which went flying into the air. That is all that happened. I felt an exhilaration, but I should not have survived it. I received the full brunt of the lightning bolt. I did not realize at the time that I had undergone some type of initiation or ancient rite of passage. For many of the tribal people of the Americas, one who is struck by lightning and survives becomes known as a lightning shaman, which they believe is the most powerful of shamanic healers. Perhaps the most extraordinary element of that experience with lightning is that not only did I survive it, but also found it exhilarating, which is almost unheard of in the indigenous cultures.

A Lakota Past Life

During this time I remembered a specific past life as a Lakota Chief and Holy Man in which I developed magic that provided protection against bullets and arrows. This particular Lakota shaman would ride on his horse back and forth in front of the soldiers, taunting them where they could fire point blank. One soldier estimated that more than a thousand rounds must have been fired directly at him. Twice his horse was shot out from beneath him, but in every case he was unharmed. When they were fighting against the Crow and other enemies, he had this same protection against arrows. This apparently was me and I had dreams of different periods in the life of this Chief.

So it would appear that I have a connection in this present life with the "thunder beings," having successfully performed multiple ceremonies to influence the weather, and probably not more than three or four times for minor situations have these ceremonies been ineffective.

This particular Lakota Chief finally died not in battle but by treachery and deceit when signing a treaty. Today, I know the person who took my life in the Lakota incarnation. He has said several times that when he sees me, he wants to burst into tears. Of course, I would never tell him what he did. In this life he has some native blood, and I have had the great honor of being the instrument for his leaving a corrupt life to become a spiritual healer.

As I have said many times in lectures and classes, I should not be here. In fact, I should not be here many times over. This has given intensity in my work. Every day I am grateful for being allowed to go on with my life when fate would have had it otherwise. It has powerfully affected my teachings and the way I live my life. I should not be here and I am living on borrowed time. This makes every moment of every day important to me, and every minute and every act takes on a quality it would not have otherwise had.

A Mysterious Adversary

More than a few times it occurred to me that in my numerous brushes with death, some of which I have not described, powerful forces did not want me to carry out my vision of calling attention to and exposing the ceiling that had been constructed over the Earth, telling people how to break through this ceiling. This was undeniable when my manuscript for Soul on Fire first lost four straight editors for odd reasons, all of whom loved the stories I had written. Then when I was accepted by a publisher, it mysteriously fell through. Then I received a call from the chief editor of another publishing company who loved my book and said he definitely wanted to publish it. My literary friends said, "When a chief editor wants it, it's a done deal." They were dead wrong. Two weeks later I received a terse notice in the mail that they were going to pass on the book, with no other explanation. This was after the chief editor had raved about the book and said he definitely wanted it.

During this twenty-four-hour period I came within inches of certain death, along with my partner, Astrid, and my stepson, who was fourteen years old at the time. This happened when a lodge pole pine snapped in a sudden afternoon storm and fell on our tent where we had scrambled for refuge from the rain. The tree missed our heads by no more than six inches and would have totally crushed us. It was only because when we heard the snapping of the tree, we raised our heads. We knew from the sound of it that we could be in grave danger, yet there was no time to react. This all happened while we were on vacation in the Grand Tetons camping at a primitive campground at Jenny Lake. The next day while making a report to a Park Service official at our camp site, I tripped over a taut chain connected to the metal bear-proof storage box in our camp site. I fell forward with dead weight, slamming my face against a jagged tree stump that was raised about six inches off the ground. There had been no time to protect myself with my arms. During the split second before I hit, both Astrid and I called upon our protection from the higher world. I survived the fall against all odds when the force should have snapped my neck like a twig or at least torn up my face and given me a severe concussion. I had several superficial gashes that quickly healed. It was truly a miraculous experience.

There was no logical explanation of how I could have avoided tragic consequences.

Going Under the Radar

I recalled Mary Summer Rain, who wrote a series of books about her experiences with an old, blind Native woman who became her teacher. Her teacher said that she literally had to "slip her book through the surveillance of the negative forces" like a snake in the grass in order to get it published. Mary Summer Rain had nearly a hundred rejections before this finally happened. I think I also had to go under the radar, because the way my book was finally published was remarkable. I did not have an agent and it was when Dr. Christiane Northrup discovered my book and felt it needed to get out to a wider audience. It was through her direct intervention that the CEO of Hay House decided to read the book. He loved it and the rest is history.

It is not paranoia when I say that there were dark forces trying at any cost to prevent me from getting my material out, even to the point of putting me in the face of death a number of times. Thank God that I had this protection brought forth from my Lakota life. I do not just give credit to that past life, but also know that today I have very powerful allies from the spiritual planes who have protected me again and again. For these angelic beings and masters, I owe my heartfelt thanks that I am able to continue my Earthly journey and my work.

I once read an episode in one of Castaneda's books in which his teacher, Don Juan, said you cannot kill a sorcerer (shaman). Castaneda asked what if someone with a high-powered rifle and a telescopic lens stayed on a mesa overlooking a road where the sorcerer walked every day at a certain time, with the avowed intention of killing the shaman. What would his teacher say to that? Don Juan shrugged his shoulders and said the shaman just would not be there at the time.

Perhaps that's how it works. I was not there when the plane crashed, and I was not there when the tree fell. Perhaps the way it works is you do not know necessarily that you are in danger every time, but because of your personal power you cause circumstances to happen where you would take a different route or not be there at that time. You might pass by early or late if that person was there with the avowed intention of killing you. It is not that you necessarily have foreknowledge, but when you are in your personal power, that power will protect you even when you do not know that you need protection.

The New Cycle: Our Direct Relationship to the Creator

Looking back to the period of awakening to the remembrance of my path, it was only in retrospect that I could see that these powers arose spontaneously, the result of being on my spiritual path and doing my spiritual practices. It was not by trying to make these things happen. Perhaps in the back of my mind I knew this was what I was supposed to do. It was my path to remember all of it, to awaken the abilities I had developed in past lives, and to demonstrate that we all have these abilities and this wisdom within us.

We all have the ability to receive knowledge directly from Creation rather than through an intermediary, whether it is a priest, rabbi, church, a temple, a mystery school, a guru, or a channeled ascended master. If you should have an opportunity with an intermediary, by all means seize it. But in the New Cycle there are going to be vast numbers of people who will be awakening and will not have this opportunity. What will they do? That is why I am demonstrating that you can accomplish what my partner and I did. You have the ability for direct contact with Creation, to go into conscious and ecstatic union with the Creator. This will be the norm in the New Cycle. The awakening will be as real as one could have working with a master teacher. Millions of seekers will be in direct contact with the Creation and the Creator.

I realize too that I assumed a number of teachers had these abilities I had been developing, and even as I speak some write eloquently about miracles. They describe the power of intention, yet they do not demonstrate these miracles. Even with some of our finest teachers, this false belief system of our being limited is deeply entrenched. In addition, the idea that we should avoid awakening these *siddhis* because they are ego-inflating and distracting can become a subtle belief system too, keeping many from awakening these abilities that are our entitlement and our birthright.

Neutralizing False Beliefs

In writing this book I intend to help lift this suppressive belief system from my fellow human beings because it has been a terrible burden for us. I remember my very first vision that most people on Earth were not able to go beyond the level of spiritual adolescence because of the suppressive belief system imposed on them. It is my intention and my desire to break through this ceiling, to demonstrate and to teach others how they too can break through the ceiling of false beliefs, and together spring the trap that keeps us bound to our Earthly prison.

I will describe many of the worst beliefs imposed upon us and how we can recognize them and neutralize them. We cannot just contradict them. If someone has grown up with a poverty consciousness, they cannot just go do a ceremony for abundance and expect abundance to flow into their lives. There is a way to neutralize or override these false beliefs rather than attempting to contradict them.

I will talk not so much about techniques to help us awaken, but about what is keeping us from awakening in this moment. Enlightenment is not something we get. *It is what we are.* It is not that we do not know the right techniques to awaken; it is because we continually do things that prevent our awakening.

Then I will discuss the keys to our freedom – ones that have worked for me and my partner, Astrid. We believe they can work as well for anyone.

Chapter 2: The New Eden

A Vision of a Future

In 1971 while still a priest in the Episcopal Church, I had a series of foreboding visions of the probable futures of humankind on Earth. I was shown that we have been very poor caregivers in the Garden of Nature and were poised to reap a bitter harvest through total environmental collapse. I was told that time was rapidly running out, but we still had a choice. I was also shown an alternative. It was a vision of a second Earth – a future Earth that had been created, in which we had ushered in a veritable paradise on Earth. In this vision I was shown that we had created a new Eden in which human beings, instead of being separated from all life on Earth, had learned to live consciously in an ecstatic union with All That Is. I had been told that, although forgotten by the world's religions, this was the true path of our human species on Earth.

Eden as a State of Consciousness That We Once Knew

Eden, I was told, was not so much a place but a state of consciousness we had once experienced here on Earth, and that each one of us carries the memory of that blissful state in our heart. And if our species, which is rapidly spiraling toward destruction, is to survive the twenty-first century, we would have to bring forth our collective unconscious memories of that paradise on Earth that we once knew.

The Historical Eden

I am not referring to the primordial, unconscious state of innocence, similar to that of the animal kingdom that we knew in a far earlier cycle. Instead, I am speaking of a much higher level of transcendence from which we fell at the end of the previous cycle 13,000 years ago. It happened during the last great civilization, which has been erased from our consciousness, and as Edgar Cayce once said, "buried beneath the slime and sediment of the ages." What that civilization was and how it came to an end is a story for a later time. However, I promise to tell it, because I have had years of detailed and spontaneous recall of that great period of light we once knew.

A Quantum Shift is Needed

Today, we must make a quantum shift into a whole new reality. This is a shift into a new way of thinking, feeling, knowing, doing and being. We can no longer be content to just be seekers of the Truth. That philosophy has a built-in recipe for failure. It can send a subliminal message that we will always be seeking the Truth but never really finding it. Instead of being seekers of the Truth, we will have to be carriers and doers of the Truth. We will have to realize that Truth is within our own being. Finally, we will have to achieve the highest expression, which is to be a living embodiment of Truth. We will need to make a shift in consciousness unlike anything in our known history. Such a shift does not mean becoming a little more Earth-friendly or a little more environmentally conscious. Instead, we must make a quantum shift into a totally new reality. We will have to usher in a veritable paradise on Earth.

Eden is a word that resonates strongly in our Collective Racial Memory. It evokes images of a Primordial Paradise. In truth, it is a divine state of consciousness we once experienced when we were in blissful harmony, not only with ourselves but with all of life on Earth.

From the Mind to the Heart Space

We carry the memory of Eden in our deep unconscious. It is found, not in the recesses of the mind, but in the secret places of the heart. The identification with the mind, which currently defines the condition of our human species on Earth, is antithetical to the experience of Eden.

In my vision I was shown that the Divine Imperative for our time is that of a return to Eden in the hearts of each of us. This may seem utterly unattainable, especially considering the short time we have. It may appear to be an impossible dream.

But the reality is that Eden is already emerging from our collective unconsciousness. Its signs are everywhere, for those of us willing to open our inner levels of perception. Remember, nothing is as it seems. There was a time in remote antiquity, in which we lived in the blissful state of unity with all life. This occurred not on some distant planet or in some nebulous dream world, but here on Earth in the previous cycle. We lived on a far higher level of awareness than we now experience. In fact, if we were transported in time to that original Eden, we might find it almost incomprehensible. In that world, we lived in the consciousness of unity rather than the consciousness of separation. We fell, however, from that unity consciousness. That is the meaning of being "cast out of the garden."

Today, the forest grows silent when man enters it. Deer and rabbits flee, the squirrels stop chattering, the birds stop singing. How can this be if the wolf is able to walk alongside the caribou herds when not on the prowl, just as the lion can walk next to the gazelle? All these creatures know when their predators' bellies are full. The living sentient forest, in its own way, recognizes that the human animal is alienated from the Creation and is an outcast. It senses that man is a threat to all life, **perhaps the greatest threat the world has ever known.**

A Return to Edenic Consciousness is Needed

Today our time of exile is coming to an end. We can now create a New Eden. Amazingly, as my partner and I can bear witness, it is attainable. Eden is a way of being in relationship with all life on this wondrous Earth. It is a relationship that fills us with an ineffable joy. It is not remote and inaccessible. It is real and in the offering, but we must reach for it. Astrid and I have discovered that it is very much within our grasp. Already in our lives we have been able to demonstrate the power and joy of this transcendental state that is emerging in more and more people we encounter.

The Real Fall from Grace

The story of the Fall is an ancestral memory of being trapped in our mind. By becoming totally identified with the thinking mind as we had at the end of the previous cycle, we lost that higher level of awareness that we once knew. It happened as a result of our becoming mesmerized by the new technology that had come to Atlantis. Before that event, we were magical beings, living in a magical world and in harmony with all life on this Earth. To provide some sense of perspective, I should point out that Atlantis was around for a 100,000 years compared to the five thousand years of our modern era. Advanced technology was gifted to the Atlanteans by the visiting star families, whose intentions were of the highest, but they failed to realize that the Atlanteans were not ready for such rapid ascent.

The flaming seraphim described in Genesis, barring man's return, is not external to us. It comes from within. There was no Deity out there that banished us from Paradise. We went into a self-imposed exile. On the level of the group mind, we sentenced ourselves as a result of something that we did. We had unlocked the secrets of the mastery of time and space. Suffice it to say, there was a war. With the knowledge and technology far in advance of what we now have access to, great damage occurred to the fabric of the space-time continuum by unleashing forces that we were unable to control. This created unstable areas like the Bermuda Triangle. However, the Bermuda Triangle is only a small portion of the damage that occurred – damage that extends far out into parts of our solar system. This rift in the fabric of space-time also opened the door for lower life forms to enter our dimension – beings whose energies were incompatible with our species. The result is that we sentenced ourselves to exile. We banished ourselves from this transcendental state to which we had evolved. We had to start over and try to get it right in the New Cycle that began 13,000 years ago. We fell in awareness down through the planes and sub-planes. Mercifully, we elected to forget the paradise that we knew.

Myths to Help Us to Remember

Nonetheless, we retained our myths to help us eventually remember. Such are the stories of the Garden of Eden, the Tower of Babel, Noah, and the Babylonian Gilgamesh epic.

Who has not felt at times a longing for some lost good? When we fell in that previous cycle, bliss turned into struggle. We fell from a heightened consciousness into unconsciousness, ignorance, and delusion. We moved from a glorious unity consciousness into the consciousness of separation. We found ourselves in a state of separation from self, from one another, and from all life on this Earth. In this separation consciousness, we forgot the universal language of spirit. We began to speak in many tongues. No longer could we communicate directly with one another or with other life forms. This is the real meaning of the Tower of Babel in the Scriptures. It is said that there was at that time "but one language, yet few words were spoken." This can only mean telepathic communication was the universal mode of communication among our species at the time.

Starting Over

We were given the opportunity to develop a more certain foundation that would enable us to return to that exalted state, but with deeper wisdom and compassion that we previously had lacked. Today that trial period is coming to an end. And now we face evolutionary pressure to force us to make a profound shift in consciousness.

Evolutionary Pressure

The evolutionary pressure is that we most likely will not survive the twenty-first century as a species with our existing invasive technology. The threat it now poses to our environment is enormous. We are threatened not just with the extinction of countless species, but that of destruction of the life support systems on Earth, which are Earth's system of checks and balances. They are Earth's auto-immune system. If enough of these are lost, our planet loses the ability to heal herself and could become another Mars.

Vision of a New Earth

I have already described my vision of a New Earth bathed in golden light. I was also shown the means of creating a New Eden on this Earth. When I set out to realize that vision in my own life, by normal standards and beliefs of our consensus reality culture, I possibly would have been considered a raving lunatic to believe I could accomplish this. And some of those around me undoubtedly perceived me in that way. But there is a type of divine insanity that transcends all judgments, labels and opinions. I felt driven, as one possessed, to pursue my quest for this New Eden – my quest for a different way of thinking, feeling, doing and being.

The Vision

I had a vision in which the ancient separation from our Earth and all life on it had been healed. We had created a new reality in which we lived in ecstatic union with all life in this world. It was a very magical world. We had learned that as we perceive our world so is our experience of our world. But it would not become possible until we had rediscovered that magic within ourselves. That is the entitlement and birthright of every human being.

This was a vision in which the forest no longer was silent when man entered. The forest creatures no longer lived in fear of us and would approach us with trust. We humans had learned the silent language of Creation and could call the animals to us, could go to them, understand them, and be in relationship with them. But it was not just animals we could communicate with. We could communicate with the consciousness of the plants and trees. We could communicate with the spirits of the great rocks and sacred sites. We had come to know the spirits of the rivers, mountains and oceans, the spirits of the desert springs and the great canyons of the Southwest. We had even learned to communicate with the Primal

Forces of Creation. The powers of Wind and Fire we called Brother, as Saint Francis once did long ago. And like Saint Francis, the powers of Water and Earth we called our sister, for we had realized that all is life and that there is awareness in everything. Most of all, we had discovered that we are beings without limitations and could consciously choose whatever we wanted to create.

Most importantly, we had come into relationship with the consciousness of the Earth herself. We had learned to recognize the Earth as a physical manifestation of a great divine Feminine Being who is responsible for all that we have and are. We had made a shift from the consciousness of separation to a unity consciousness. We no longer just took from our Earth; we had learned to give back.

We had come to understand it was not just we who needed Nature, for beauty, healing, nurturing, food and companionship, but Nature needed us. It was through our love and appreciation that the plants and animals came to realize their own specialness and had become self-aware, which is the destiny of all Nature on this Earth. We had learned at last that Earth is not something to own, divide, buy and sell. And that the Earth did not belong to us, but that we belonged to the Earth.

Imagine: Peace with the World!

Most people are familiar with John Lennon's powerful and moving song, Imagine, written during the height of the Vietnam War. Implicit in the lyrics is that we consider what it would be like to have World Peace. On some level this talented bard understood the enormous power of our imagination to create a new reality. I would like to challenge you to imagine a different kind of peace – to imagine that we have made peace with the Earth and all Life on it. We cannot have real peace in our world apart from being at peace with our world and with ourselves. We cannot end wars among humans without ending the war with the Earth that a number of our species are engaged in.

It is not that some people are deliberately making war with the Earth, but the effect of the exploitation of the Earth and rape of her resources out of greed is the same as if we had declared war on our world.

It is a war we cannot possibly win, because we are part of our world and not separate from Her. Our beloved Earth is not ours to divide up, parcel out, buy and sell or to own, as we have been brought up to believe, because, contrary to much contemporary thought, Earth does not belong to us; we belong to the Earth.

This kind of misconception is what caused the native people of this land to find the Europeans almost incomprehensible. They could not comprehend the new arrivees' concept of ownership of land. I have spoken often of a universal law that is recognized by all indigenous peoples, but which we have largely forgotten: "When you take something, whether from a person or a natural area, you give back in return, something of equal or greater value." Sadly, and to our peril, we have just taken more and more from the Earth without giving back. Therefore, there can be no "peace on Earth, good will toward men," unless we are at peace with the Earth and demonstrate good will toward all Life on it.

The outer world in which we dwell is a mirror of the world within us. It has been said, "As above, so below, as without, so within." When there is widespread pollution of our rivers, lakes and seas, it is because we have toxic feelings and emotions. That is always the case. When the atmosphere is polluted, it reflects the toxic nature of our thoughts. When the Earth is full of harmful and poisonous chemicals and bacterial waste, it is a reflection of what we take into our bodies.

Any attempt to clean up our environment will utterly fail until we have purified our bodies, emotions and minds. So I ask you to image a life in which you have achieved total harmony with our world and with yourself.

Imagine a world in which you are able to walk into a forest without that forest growing silent as a result of your presence. In fact, it would seem as if the chorus of birds and the chattering of squirrels would grow louder, as if rejoicing in your presence.

Imagine walking through a meadow and feeling the energy fields of the trees, shrubs and flowers reach out to embrace you as you walk by.
Imagine an incandescent glow around the flowers and foliage, which increases as you walk by.

Imagine being able to read the invisible landscape of a woodland and knowing its history and who lives there.

Imagine being able to call in a cooling breeze on a hot summer day when you are camping, or to call up a storm to end a drought, or to stop a torrential downpour on the highway when your wipers do not work.

Imagine you are able to almost instantly stop a thirty-mile-per-hour wind that had been blowing day and night for four days, because that same wind is driving a forest fire down a canyon toward you and your group of vision questers.

Imagine having a deer approach you and drop to its knees ten feet away, gazing up at you in complete trust. Or to have a doe standing on a trail ahead of you as if waiting for your arrival and also drop to her knees when you are less than a few paces away.

Imagine having a dove fly out of the trees and begin plucking at your shoelaces and then attempt to nest in your hair.

Imagine being able to call wild animals to you, including bears, a bison herd, deer, coyotes, a black snake, red-tail hawks and eagles.

Imagine while in a wilderness area being able to approach and join a very skittish herd of bighorn sheep and being accepted by them. You then invite them to join you at your campsite and, to your amazement, the next morning you see the entire herd has made the three-mile journey to your campsite of vision questers.

Imagine approaching a deer and her young fawn, and her allowing you to reach out and touch them both. You then invite them to come to your tent nearly a mile away, and to your great joy, they are there at first light, grazing in front of your tent.

Imagine warning a family of deer that it is hunting season and that they would be protected by remaining close to your home. That evening they show up at the steps of your porch, with one actually calling to you, and they remain, joined by others, throughout hunting season.

Imagine calling a long-vanished species back into your area, and several weeks later it announces its presence to you after over a hundred years' absence.

Imagine using your intention to clear the dense pollution out of your area for nearly two weeks over a radius of thirty miles. You are blessed with cobalt skies and spring-like temperatures in spite of the fact that it is summer. Then for the next four years you repeat this several times with similar success.

Imagine being able to negotiate with some destructive wood bees and a colony of yellow jackets that have invaded your home, and they are gone in an hour.

Imagine while camping alone in the Utah outback, hearing the wind whisper a message that saves your life. Or hearing the whisper of a tiny cedar shrub growing out of a rock outcropping giving you a message that resolves a health crisis.

Imagine the joy of discovery that there is a deep awareness in all of Nature and that you can communicate with any part of it and feel, hear and know its response to you.

Finally, imagine the unbelievable discovery of a lifetime that you yourself are not the limited being that your mentors described to you when you were a child. Imagine you no longer are bound to laws of the physical plane; you are, in fact, a being whose essential nature is without limitations of any kind.

I have just described some of the highlights of the spiritual journeys of my wife Astrid and me. This is a life that you also can live, not in some distant lifetime or as some remote ideal that can never be attained. This is a life of joy beyond words in which you have achieved a state of ecstatic union with the whole of Creation. It is our promise to you that this incredible gift can be yours as well in the here and now. Far from our having an "exclusive" on this joyous and expanded way of life, you too can learn to experience and share this life of almost incomprehensible bliss and unspeakable joy.

My Promise to You

I will tell you this, and this is my promise to you: If you surrender to your Earth Goddess, she in turn will surrender to you, bestowing on you gifts and blessings beyond measure. With the patriarchal takeover and the suppression of the Feminine, our world has largely forgotten Her, with the exception of the indigenous peoples of every land. And this has led us to the brink of destruction. Yet one of the most amazing things about the Earth spirit is that she never coerces. She allows! Because she respects your most precious gift from our Creator, which is freedom of will.

Our Earth Mother has never forgotten you, and in fact knows each of you by name. Can you believe that? This Exalted Being knows you by name, and not only knows your name, but knows all about you, better than you know yourselves? She has never forgotten you, even though you have forgotten her. She does not need to be worshipped, just remembered and acknowledged and appreciated as our Primal Feminine Source of Life and as the One who is responsible for all that we have and are. She wants what any human woman wants: for you to be in relationship with her and stay connected. We are the real prodigal children that are finally returning home again. In that still place in your heart, she continually calls you, as part of herself, to herself. She draws you, but does not demand; she calls, but does not compel.

A Living Embodiment of the New Eden

I discovered that creating a new Eden in our world was quite possible, and was a key to a truly ecstatic life. I realized that Astrid, my much younger but enormously talented partner, was able to achieve this joyous and ecstatic state in ten years, a feat that took me several decades. This is not to say that her journey is completed – for both of us it is still a work in progress. And we are continually expanding the parameters of this new consciousness that has become the focal point of our lives. Of course, Eden is not a place but an ecstatic state of being in harmony with all life. It is what happens to us when we move from the mind, which by its very nature creates duality and therefore separation, to the heart that knows only unity and oneness. I have said to my students: "When through the mind we try to achieve something good, evil comes in, usually unnoticed, by the back door. For example, our prohibition laws which were an attempt to do away with the evils of alcohol, enabled organized crime to gain a foothold in America for the first time."

A Command over the Winds and Water

A few years ago Astrid and I were with a group of nine adults who had joined us outside of Canyonlands National Park for a week-long vision quest. But our story had begun two days before our group arrived. We had come early to prepare the land that was to be our base camp.

As always we set up an energetic boundary to keep away unwanted energies and campers who would not be in tune with our philosophy. In the past, this procedure had proved amazingly effective. With summer almost upon us, it was quite hot and we did something we had done at other times: We called up the Wind spirits to give us a cooling breeze for our quest. Our surprise was not that it happened, but the speed and intensity of the wind's response. Although we had demonstrated this command over of the Winds on other occasions, within several minutes a thirty-five-mile-per-hour wind was blowing and continued uninterrupted day and night for the next four days.

56

We did not complain. The wind was a balm for us, which provided relief from the intense heat of Utah's high desert and canyon country.

On the fourth night, which was the second night after our vision questers had arrived, we were startled to perceive a glow several miles up the canyon from where we had our base camp. The glow quickly became brighter. Within minutes we smelled the smoke, and then the ashes began falling on us. We realized that a forest fire was rapidly approaching us as the wind was funneling directly down the canyon. We knew we could get ourselves out, but we would lose everything as there was no time to take our tents, sleeping bags, food and supplies. A stream ran through the middle of this half-mile to mile-wide canyon, and there was much dry vegetation, including large cottonwood trees that would go up like tinder. However, I was inspired to try an alternative to making a quick escape. Since I was in the midst of cooking stir-fried veggies for our group, I asked Astrid to intervene by calling in the Wind devas to stop the winds from blowing the fire that was rapidly being propelled toward us. I told her that I did not want our dinner to get burned. She laughed and agreed to do this with the help of two of our vision questers. She faced the wind to make contact with the Wind elementals. I knew she was up to the job.

Astrid's Achievements

I had witnessed Astrid stop a torrential downpour when we were on an interstate and discovered that the windshield wipers were broken. Recently while camping in the northern Rockies in a primitive camping area, I watched her call up the Winds on an unusually hot afternoon. Even though I knew Astrid had developed a "command" over the elements as had I, still I was impressed at her obvious power. I was amazed that seconds later there was a sound in the distance that got louder and louder. I then realized it was the approaching wind. Finally the lodge pole pines overhead were waving wildly.

Sometimes, even I am amazed at her abilities. The previous summer, we had been experiencing a drought in eastern Tennessee, and I suggested she call in a wild thunderstorm, but she insisted we needed a female rain. This is a Navaho term for a soft, gentle, continual rain that soaks into the land and nurtures all Nature.

Passing on the Mantle

Over the last three decades I had performed numerous rain ceremonies to end droughts or flooding in different parts of the country. Some of these were accomplished at a distance. Now it was time to pass on the mantle. I enjoyed watching Astrid do the ceremonies, because she had become the living embodiment of this new Eden that I had envisioned. She was the perfect testimonial to my claim that we all have these powers within us.

It is only our beliefs that separate us from these powers that are our birthright. I felt Astrid represented our future. She represents where we have to go as a species.

Astrid got her female rain within forty-eight hours. It lasted for five days. We listened to the soft, gentle rain day and night until finally she said, "Okay, that's enough." The rain stopped within an hour, and the drought in eastern Tennessee had ended. I love her naturalness and I believe our friends of the elemental world love it also.

A Modern Female Saint Francis

Astrid has been referred to by some as a modern female Saint Francis and I concur, even though she refuses to accept that designation. On several occasions while camping in the Rockies, I have watched deer approach her and, instead of running off when they got near, drop to their knees only ten feet away, and gaze at her in complete trust. In my book, Soul on Fire, I describe the time a wild dove flew out of the forest and began pecking at Astrid's shoe laces and then ended up trying to nest in her hair. Fortunately, we had a camera with us that enabled us to capture this magical moment.

It was during the same camping trip that Astrid stated her intention to be visited by bears, which are her totem animals. In the days ahead, bears kept appearing out of nowhere, crossing back and forth in front of us. This happened within hours of stating her intention. It happened in Wyoming and two weeks later in California, and then when we returned home to Tennessee. It seemed to make no difference where we were. There was no doubt in my mind that she had been in direct communication with the Bear Oversoul.

During this camping trip in western Wyoming, we both had experiences of spotting a herd of about fifty buffalo across the prairie approximately half a mile away. We remarked to each other how we wished they'd come to us. No more than thirty seconds later, the head matriarch of the herd rose up and began moving toward us. We could not believe our eyes. The rest of the herd fell into single-file behind her. In this case we were not trying to "call" them. We were reminded that once the power of intention has been awakened, there is great power in the spoken word. They came over and crossed the narrow Forest Service road, where we were parked only yards away. And then as if to say, "Okay, we came to visit as you requested, but we like it better where we were," they turned, walked back single-file and continued grazing and basking in the afternoon sun at the exact spot where we had seen them.

In *Soul on Fire*, I have told a number of stories of my magical experiences with animals and plants as well as my command over the elements. But here was another person who was transcending the false beliefs of the times, doing the same thing. One of the most exciting demonstrations of Astrid's sense of unity with the natural world occurred when we were visiting the Red Rock Canyons in central Utah.

A Dome of Protection

One summer a situation arose when we had to make a fifteen-mile drive in the dark on a country road in Utah. It turned out there were hundreds of mule deer and rabbits grazing along this stretch on the shoulders of the road. Unfortunately, when our headlights hit them, they were blinded and would often jump in front of the automobile at the last minute. It was a harrowing drive, and we actually hit a couple of rabbits and narrowly missed several deer. This was an open range, and so there were several times when we would turn on a curve and there would be cattle. Astrid, who was driving, was extremely upset, especially about hitting the rabbits and almost hitting the deer. But she came up with a solution. The next several nights when we had to make the same drive she asked the Nature devas to keep them safe. Next she stated her intention to place a protective dome of light over the entire stretch of road.

It was an amazing thing to watch. Not a single one of the hundreds of rabbit, deer and cattle that were grazing on the side of the road ever set foot on the pavement when we drove by. Even more incredible, on several occasions while Astrid was driving, we saw a rabbit or deer that would panic and attempt to leap in front of our car only to hit an invisible wall and be stopped in midair. It was such a joyous experience to be able to protect these beautiful little beings. She has since used this protective "dome" on other occasions, always with positive results.

The Beginner's Mind

What is more amazing to me than the special encounters with wild creatures is the childlike wonder and even rapture that Astrid experiences whenever she encounters any creature, no matter how tiny, or even a lone flower growing on the side of the road.

When we first got together, I had to adjust to my wife urgently calling me to her garden to observe a tiny lizard, dragonfly or praying mantis, or while driving, for her to suddenly swerve onto the shoulder without warning and jump out to observe a single flower growing on a hillside, a sunset, a rainbow, or the way the sun was filtering through the trees.

More than anyone I know, she exhibits the Buddhist's idea of the "beginner's mind." Every experience, every encounter with the natural world is as if it were the first. The joyous wonder and openness to the world at large is something that I have seen in Astrid many times. Those who know her are aware of her uninhibited, childlike quality, but they are not fooled for, they know that she carries within her the wisdom of the ages. Once while walking with her along a cascading stream that flows out of the Smoky Mountain National Park, I heard what appeared to be an audible voice saying how blessed I was to be with a "blonde" Sophia. I asked around to see who was speaking, but of course no one was there.

An Infallible Testimonial

I do know this: If you wish to get an indication of how far along you are in your development, observe how animals and small children are around you. If they are continually drawn to you like a magnet wherever you happen to be, then you can be sure that this positive testimonial is more valid than that of the most renowned and esteemed teachers. Those teachers' judgments, wise as they are, are fallible, but that tiny child who is drawn to you or that little four-legged creature or feathered creature that comes to you without fear – their judgment is infallible. By contrast I have seen some acknowledged teachers or writers of spiritual philosophy that have little rapport with animals or children. Although I would not judge them, I know that I would never seek out their counsel.

The Power of Laughter

Please remember what I said earlier: Rather than describing some abstract ideal of what Edenic consciousness is, I have chosen to use the example of a real-life, flesh-and-blood person – a person I know more than anyone else in the world.

An amazing expression of Astrid's Edenic consciousness is her perpetual lightness and laughter. Recently, the Dalai Lama asked the question, what was enlightenment? He smiled broadly with a twinkle in his eye and said, "Lighten up! It means lighten up!" And then, "You have to lighten up," he repeated again. When I heard this, I realized he could have been describing Astrid.

Her laughter is never at another's expense, but is totally natural, spontaneous, infectious, and sometimes even riveting and compulsive. It seems to erupt at the slightest provocation. This seemingly inexhaustible fountain of laughter that she carries is a natural outgrowth of the sheer joy that she experiences with all life. I believe that it is this attitude that will help catapult our species into the next level in the coming decades. Those who know her say they have never seen anyone who laughed so much. I would have to agree. Almost anything seems to move her to laughter. She sees humor in everything. Sometimes I have to stretch to see what is so funny about a particular situation, and yet her joy fills me so much that it really does not matter.

Considering that Astrid has known considerable pain and heartache in her life, it makes the laughter even more remarkable and valid. She has used stumbling blocks in her life as stepping stones and as tools for transformation. She has used laughter to heal and has even been able to pass it on to others.

A few years ago I saw her use this gift with a particular client who never smiled and always appeared unhappy. Every time we saw this client, she was overly heavy and serious. She carried an aura of sadness that she could never fully let go of. Somehow in the course of ordinary conversation with Astrid, I saw her go into uncontrollable laughter. They both erupted into this riveting laughter that lasted about fifteen minutes. Those of us around were amazed to see what was happening. We wondered how she had done it. The woman was transformed by the experience. She is now simply a joy to be around. Since that time I have seen Astrid pass on her gift of "holy laughter" (as this high *siddhi* is sometime referred to) to others who needed to "lighten up."

One of the most remarkable demonstrations of humor is when Astrid has been speaking with total strangers on the phone. On a number of occasions I have heard her talking on the phone to solicitors and creditors (the kind of people that most of us want to hang up on), but within minutes she had them in uncontrollable laugher. I do not know how she does it, but I know she made the day for those people.

An Amazing Healing

The episode that really stands out in my mind, however, is when we were in Asheville, North Carolina, doing a healing out of our motel room. One particular woman, it turned out, had a serious possession. We were encountering difficulty getting this reluctant and very negative spirit to leave. The woman herself was almost comatose. I should not have had to worry, because my partner managed to get the possessed woman to shift into riveting laughter. That was too much, even for the negative spirit. It was unable to withstand the high vibration of laughter. It had to leave its nest. I have wondered if this was the first time in the history of the planet that laugher was used as a method for de-possession. One master has said that "laughter is far more powerful than either prayer or meditation". It was a German mystic, Meister Eckhart, who wrote about laughter, saying this is the "very essence of the Creation." He said that laughter is what brings the Creation into being: "God laughed, and there was a universe." He meant by this that laughter contains within it the vibrations of joy, compassion, gratitude, appreciation, harmony, spontaneity, and many of the things that we feel are the gifts of the spirit.

Joy and Ecstatic Union

Whether in the world of Nature or with people, Astrid seems always to be totally present. **Astrid's holy laughter comes out of her deep expression of ecstatic joy of all life. This is her gift to the world. She serves joy.** Joy is different from happiness in that happiness is dependent on good things happening to us, dependent on getting what we want. Joy has nothing to do with what happens to us, nothing to do with our external life. It is a state of consciousness that is independent of the externals of life. I am referring to the Edenic consciousness – a state of being in ecstatic union with all that is. This is the true, though forgotten past and destiny of our species. It is a path that must be embraced by humanity in this century. To be in ecstatic union is to be liberated from the tyranny of the egoic mind.

Edenic Consciousness: Doorway to Enlightenment

So if I say that Astrid has come to embody Edenic consciousness, do I mean that she never gets upset or frustrated or angry? The answer is no! Does she sometimes make choices that are not for her highest good, choices that do not best serve her? The answer is yes! If you expect to find someone exhibiting a kind of perfection, best keep your sense of humor with you, because you will need it when around her. But if you mean that my partner is not controlled by these human emotions, does not indulge or wallow in them, but quickly throws them off just as a healthy body quickly throws off toxins, then you can decide by my description of her and see for yourself. As far as I can tell, the most advanced beings in our world today are far from impervious to the emotional, mental and psychic toxins that are part of the condition of our present humanity, but they quickly throw them off, refusing to indulge in them for a single minute.

Chapter 3: A Return to Magic

Not long ago, I ran into Kate, a woman who apprenticed with me in the late '80s and early '90s. She was in fact the same person who had assisted me with the rain ceremony in northern Arizona in February in the early '90s that brought in the next morning, totally unforecasted, the storm of the decade, dumping many feet of snow in the San Francisco Peaks, thus ending a two-and-a-half year drought.

Kate was part of an international group of apprentices from the U.S., Mexico, Canada and Alaska. The group would get together for four-day weekends in spring, winter and fall and for ten days in July, at a base camp on the Gros Ventre River that adjoined Grand Teton National Park. Ordinarily, our "gatherings" were encampments in wilderness areas, except in winter, when we met in my home in Highlands, North Carolina. This was, in fact, the home that had been made financially possible through a Memphis woman named Edith, who wished to express her gratitude in a very tangible way for the spontaneous healing of uterine cancer she experienced years earlier when she had come to me for help.

After playing "catch-up," Kate said, "The thing I remember most when I was with you is that magic just seemed to follow you around. We all felt it was such an honor to be with you, to be brought into your world, and to be a part of what you were attempting to 'create.' I have missed that terribly, for it seemed that all that magic left me when we disbanded."

Kate indeed had seen many wonders when she was part of my far-flung group of apprentices. I clearly remember how each time we would gather for teaching or ceremonies, an eagle would appear circling overhead, no matter in what part of the country we were. Sometimes it would be a pair, and other times a fledgling would join the parents. Some of the group would even try to guess how long it would be before the first eagle appeared and from which direction. Many of our group, which averaged eighteen to twenty people at any given time, also had strong connections with eagles, and we ended up referring to ourselves as "The Eagle Clan." It seemed to fit us.

I remember other occasions, when Kate was with us, telling some of our group that we would be able to see a bear at a particular location at a specific time. We were never disappointed. As if by appointment, our bear would show up within minutes on the other side of a marshy meadow of willow stands. We kept a respectful distance, of course. These were extraordinary experiences of being in sync with the natural world.

We were an ecstatic group. Our pow-wows were incredible outpourings of our spirits with much singing, chanting, music, dancing and drumming. We all brought drums, flutes, guitars, rattles and even a didgeridoo. Four of our men had been professional drummers and musicians and would lead us into magical rhythms accompanied by chanting. Several of our women had lovely voices. One woman had been a Broadway singer. She had the voice of an angel, but she also often shifted into very primal sounds that one would expect of tribal people.

While all these memories were passing in review before my mind, I said to Kate, "I'm so sorry that you feel you have lost that magic we all shared. I know now that magic is not something we can get. It's who we are. We are the magic, and we must look within to find it, not outside of ourselves. You have never lost anything. You just did not know where to look. But now you know."

I have shared Kate's description of her own experience as well as others who were with us, because I believe she reflected a deep unconscious longing that many have. Most would not have been able to articulate that longing, however, because they have not had the same opportunities. Still, I have become aware of the feeling many have that there is something very vital missing in their lives as they move robot-like about their daily activities.

A Separation from our Essential Nature

We are indeed magical beings living in a magical world which is part of a magical, non-local, infinite Creation. Deep down, we all know what is right and true. That is our essential nature. But with the shift we made eons ago from our heart-space, feeling nature, to identification with our mind, we lost that capacity. We fell into a state of separation. Thinking replaced knowing. We began to distrust our deeper feelings about life. Whereas formerly we had acted out of our knowing, now we shifted to the sequence of knowing-thinking-doing. We feared making any choice, executing any action without having to think about it. Suddenly the mind had to be in control, to monitor, pass judgment, and edit all that welled up out of our deep, intuitive, knowing ature. And so our natural access to our true feeling was lost. Thus we lost the ability to seize the moment, to act with empowerment, because the mind had taken control. It had to be totally in charge – it feared intuition and feeling and knowing. In short, it separated us from our essential nature.

The mind is masculine; knowing, feeling, and intuition are feminine. One can readily see how this shift to a patriarchal takeover resulted in the Divine Feminine being swept aside. Knowing this, one could almost have predicted a Holocaust, as well as the systematic executions throughout Europe and America of what some historians have estimated as twenty million women and children during the centuries of persecution, inquisitions,
witch hunts and heresy trials. Under the tyranny of the mind, which unlike our feeling nature is not a soul function, we had moved onto a dark path of struggle, suffering and confusion.

And of course, there is the systematic slaughter of indigenous peoples around the world, as well as the destruction of their way of life. And here in our own country, while we have hypocritically pointed the finger at the German people, few know that genocide of our own indigenous people was the official policy of our government for a time – or that, to carry out this policy, blankets riddled with small pox were passed out to thousands of Native Americans, resulting in the decimation of entire villages. At this time there was the successful attempt to wipe out the buffalo, the main food source for the Western Tribes. But history is written by the winners, and few Americans today are aware of what really happened.

The point I am making is that the mind, when separated from the feeling nature, becomes a tyrant. However, when tempered and balanced by our feeling, intuitive, knowing natures, the mind will become a valuable tool for our transformation and evolution as a species, as it is destined to be when we have made the shift into Unity Consciousness in the New Cycle that is being ushered in.

To speak of ourselves as magical beings is another way of saying that we are beings without limitations.

There is great resistance to the above idea among many. It seems part of us wants the status quo, or we do not want to believe we can do better, or that we are living limited lives because of our resistance to a new way of perceiving ourselves.

Shaman Stories

Now I will to share some stories that could be considered demonstrations of our ability to transcend the laws of the physical plane, which in isolation prove little, but taken as a body along with other references in this text, provide cumulative evidence that we indeed are beings without limitations.

The stories my partner and I are sharing are what could be called "shaman stories," because they are episodes involving magical encounters with the World of Nature that are true, yet transcend the "known" laws of our physical third dimensional life here on Earth. Because of this, they carry a certain power and potential (not found in other kinds of stories) to bring about personal transformation. They nudge what in some Native American traditions is known as the "second attention," which is our awareness of the inner worlds. These can only be perceived by our "inner senses." By contrast, the first attention is our awareness of the outer worlds perceived by our physical senses on which the majority of our species is fixated at this time. There is an illusory quality in this fixation on the outer worlds, and as a result most remain trapped in this illusion. In addition, these shaman stories evoke deep soul memories of who we really are. Usually, however, these memories come forth more as feelings and a sense of empowerment rather than as specific information. There is a timelessness about such stories with the capacity to touch people's lives more deeply than the conscious mind can fathom. They can touch a person regardless of their ethnic or religious background.

The many stories about our experiences with our animal friends, plant spirits and those of the elemental or energetic world are not just to entertain you with amazing stories but to open you to a different way of perceiving the world and to the idea that we are part of a "conscious creation," that there is a deep awareness in all life around us. And that it is an experience of ecstatic joy to surrender to the Earth and experience a conscious union with the spirits of animals, plants and the stones themselves – with the consciousness of a forest or mountain or a river spirit, or the spirit of a canyon, a desert spring or a great grandmother tree. Our Ascension is inseparably connected to our return and complete surrender to Gaia, our Earth Mother. I know this is hard to accept when we are immersed in the hi-tech world of our time and polarized in our masculine rational mind. I know of no other way of putting it; that is why I am going to such lengths to explain these concepts. It is because our (and humanity's) surrender to Earth will be our Ascension.

I have written about one of my early visions while still a priest in the Episcopal Church, in which I was told I was to awaken the spiritual talents I had gained in other lifetimes, and then be able to demonstrate these as a small part of the powers latent in all of us. I was told that this would help to awaken such abilities in others, and their demonstrations in turn would inspire others.
I was told that, to my astonishment, only a very small percentage of the human population would need to make this "shift," in order for it to become part of our DNA for the whole of humanity. Then everyone to some extent would get it, even though they would not know why. This, in turn, would be tantamount to a major paradigm shift into an awareness that each one of us is a manifestation of our One Creator. We would come to understand that we indeed are inherently beings without limitations.

I have also stated that once I had made my leap from the protective canopy of mainstream religion into the uncharted waters of Spirit, it seemed as if my whole life was orchestrated by some mysterious, guiding Power. Again and again, it seemed as if seldom a week went by that I was not called upon to demonstrate the limitlessness of who we truly are as divine beings. Sometimes I was aware of what I was being called to do – ever inspired by the words of a great master and avatar: "These things and more shall you be able to do!"

At others times it just seemed as if I were thrust into the midst of a challenging situation and wanted to resolve it. Only in retrospect was I able to perceive this as part of a script that had already been written.

The following anecdotes perhaps capture the wide diversity of what I was experiencing.

Lost at "Three Forks"

During the first year of my separation from my former partner, I was feeling totally lost and without direction. This situation in my personal life was reflected to me by our "mirror universe" in an unmistakable way on a day when I decided to drive over to a trailhead in the Nantahala National Forest near my home in Highlands, North Carolina. The mile-and-a-half of almost overgrown path led to a place known as the Three Forks, where there was an impressive confluence of three large streams.

I began around mid-afternoon, bringing with me sandwiches and a little fruit. Upon reaching my destination, I found myself exhilarated by the cascading streams, waterfalls and large, deep pools. It was well worth the effort. After exploring a bit, I swam and then stretched out on my towel to bask in the mid-afternoon August sun. I awoke several hours later, experiencing complete disorientation and near panic. For a moment I had no idea where on Earth I was. It was completely dark, and a thick cloud covering along with the dense canopy of trees made for zero visibility. I could not even see my hand in front of me. I had no flashlight or matches. I knew I could not spend the night there in only shorts and a cotton shirt, as the late August evenings in the Blue Ridge Mountains can be quite cool. Besides, I knew rain was imminent.

For about thirty minutes, I stumbled about like a blind person, trying to locate the trail, fighting rapidly increasing panic. What was I to do?

Then a sudden calm settled over me, and almost immediately I found what I knew must be the trail; but without any visibility, how would I be able to stay on it? After moving very cautiously and losing the trail several times, I seemed to fall into some kind of rhythm. I did not realize at the time that I had shifted into heightened awareness.

I stepped up the pace without realizing I was moving faster than when I had come in under full daylight. At one point, I sensed that I was approaching the large white pine that had fallen across the trail. After crawling for perhaps ten yards, I could feel the trunk of the tree pushing against my back, and I knew I had intuited correctly. At that time, it never occurred to me to wonder how I was able to accomplish this feat.

Finally, to my relief, I reached the trailhead where I had parked my car. It was only then I realized that whereas I had stumbled several times coming in on the narrow, rough trail, I did not even break my pace coming out. Besides, I had moved at a faster pace without sight.

Then there was the sudden realization of what I had just accomplished. I was in awe. Somehow without physical eyesight, I had used another faculty for "seeing." It was as if some atavistic trait we once had, that may have been necessary for survival, had been activated.

In yet another way, I discovered that we are in no way limited by physical plane laws, and that we truly have the ability to "see" without eyes, "hear" without ears and "know" without thought.

In addition to that realization, I perceived a lesson for my current condition. If I tried to rely on my rational mind to find my way through the mental and emotional maze I was in, then I would utterly fail. However, if I trusted my inner senses, then I could move down my path through life with ease and assurance.

Bird Woman of Ft. Lauderdale

In the mid-80s I was invited to do workshops by a group based in South Florida. My former partner and I were the guests of a woman who had a home on a large lake outside of Ft. Lauderdale. While we were eating dinner at her home on the first night, she shared with us a problem which recently had arisen. For years she had set out feeding stations and fruit trees to attract many different species of birds. She had come to love their presence and their calls and songs. In time there were birds that would come right up to her and eat out of her hand whenever she ventured into her yard.

Then about two weeks before my arrival an ominous silence filled her yard, and the sounds of her birds abruptly ceased. It was a real-life Rachel Carson "Silent Spring." Suspicious, she discovered that her neighbor had acquired three large felines that had staked out her yard. She was at a loss of what to do. She missed her birds terribly.

Her request to us was could we help her bring back her birds. We agreed to try, but had no idea exactly what to do.

"Oh, and could you also help me bring back Boa and Zoa?" she added. This second request caused me to feel a certain trepidation. "Who or what," I asked, "were Boa and Zoa?"

"Boa and Zoa were my two six-foot boa constrictors," she continued. "They disappeared six months ago when our lake was sprayed. I do not even know if they are still alive, but I miss them."

Hearing all of this, I wondered if she realized what she was asking of us, but we agreed to try. We went out that afternoon to a place in her yard that seemed appropriate, and after making tobacco offerings we explained to the Nature elements what we wished to do.

We then called in a great horned owl to be protector of the birds, knowing that with one of these magnificent birds around no cat would show itself. We then asked the elementals to round up Boa and Zoa and bring them back.

The next morning the birds were back, chirping away. Our friend was elated that our ceremony had worked, but she had no idea what we had done. "Oh, by the way," she added, "the oddest thing happened. There was an owl outside my bedroom window calling all night. How strange – I have never heard a single owl since I moved here five years ago."

Of course, we could hardly contain ourselves that our ceremony had worked so swiftly and effectively. Being cat lovers, we hoped the cats were unharmed, and just keeping their distance. We were not about to ask.

Boa and Zoa showed up two weeks later, acting as if they'd never been gone. I suppose it took a while for the Nature elementals to convince them to return, since they'd probably been traumatized by the spraying. I sensed that their neighbors might not share her elation about Boa and Zoa.

I thought how much I love my life and would never trade it for anything else. I was deeply aware of the growing euphoria of discovering the possibilities of a life without limitation and the opportunity to share this incredible truth with others. Perhaps there would be ways to help people be free of this prison without walls and break through the almost impenetrable "ceiling" that covers our Earth.

Shifting the Water Flow

Shortly after moving into our newly acquired contemporary log chalet bordering the Smokey Mountain National Park in eastern Tennessee, Astrid and I discovered we had a serious problem with our large basement apartment flooding whenever it rained. The house had been built at the end of several hundred feet of sloping land, so that the apartment was partially underground. Apparently the ground water had nowhere else to go except toward this dug-out part.

Worse still, all estimates to fix the problem were prohibitive, running into many thousands of dollars. Consequently we had no alternative but to stop using this much-needed three-hundred-fifty-square-foot space until we had the money. After two years of further flooding, I received guidance that there was another way to deal with this problem, illogical as it seemed. I went out and spoke with the Water and Earth elementals, explaining the situation and what we needed, which was nothing less than changing the direction in which the ground water drained. I made my usual offering of tobacco and expressed my gratitude and appreciation for all that they'd done for me in the past.

End of problem. To my amazement, for the next several years, not even one drop seeped through the walls or floor. Even after several torrential rains, this partially underground space was not even damp. Amazingly, however, when we made the decision to put our house up for sale and relocate, the problem re-emerged. Apparently the "blocks" that had been put in place, at my request, were then lifted.

9-1-1 Emergency

It was during the above time period that Astrid developed aspiration, the result of a minute bit of food that went into her lungs, setting up infection. Antibiotics were prescribed, but she was unable to tolerate them. They made her violently ill. So we attempted to treat her infection in our way, using some natural antibiotics that were not invasive. During the second night of her infection I was up all night with her, watching closely to see if she was getting any fluid in her lungs. Several times it appeared that she was beginning to fill with fluid, and I felt strongly we should call 911. But Astrid refused, in her weakened state still believing she would get better.

Finally around three o'clock in the morning there was a change for the better, and by morning she was past her crisis. Around mid-afternoon there was a knock on the door, and when I opened it, I was shocked to see two police officers from 911 – a day late and a dollar short.

They claimed they'd received a call from someone at this number around two o'clock in the morning and had called back, but no one answered. I explained our situation and that I came close to calling but did not. One of them laughed, saying we must have a psychic telephone (little did they know). He insisted, however, that he had a male voice on tape and again correctly repeated our phone number. It turned out that their call back was on our answering machine, but for some reason the phone had never rung.

Perhaps this is an extraordinary example of the unlimited possibilities of the powers of intention. To this day both of us wish we had listened to the voice that was captured on tape. It might have been the first time one had had the opportunity to listen to the voice of their double.

I'm Going to Give You Back Your Voice

Another extraordinary story that comes to mind involved Astrid and me running into a former apprentice of mine, whom I had not seen for fifteen years. He reminded me of a healing he had experienced through me when I had last seen him years earlier. I had come by to visit Robert in his home in western North Carolina a few weeks after he'd been involved in an automobile accident. He'd been thrown against the steering wheel, severely and permanently damaging his larynx, resulting in a loss of his voice. He could only speak in a whisper. Robert was a song writer and guitarist, so his personal loss was great.

At one point, I had walked over to Robert, stating that I was going to give his voice back. I then touched his larynx and, amazingly, his voice was instantly restored. Without thinking, I had responded to a deep knowing and had seized that tiny window of opportunity.

The Creation Had to Deliver

We live in a mirror universe in which everything outside of us not only reflects us, but the Creation actually adjusts and adapts itself to us. A good example of this is an experience I had with my daughter by my first marriage. I had driven from my home in Highlands to Atlanta to pick up Rebekah for the weekend. During the last hour of the drive, it had turned dark, and I began to speak with Rebekah, who was thirteen at the time, about one of our areas of mutual interest, our love of animals.

While Rebekah was growing up, her mother had repeatedly spoken to her about my "crazy beliefs," so I had to use caution. We agreed that it was possible to communicate with animals through the mind, as she was a champion horseback rider and felt she had been in communication with Dancer, her favorite horse. But when I suggested that it was possible to call wild animals to us, as well as know where they were, her response was "no way" was that possible, and that I was teasing her.

Without flinching I ventured, "Okay, Rebekah, when we make this next turn, there'll be a deer on our right." Moments later, while going around a curve, we saw the doe, as if by appointment, standing on our right only ten feet from the road.

My daughter cried out with excitement and, of course, wanted to know how I knew. I had no answer that I could give her, but this shared experience enabled me, for the first time, to bring my daughter into my magical world. This experience went beyond clairvoyance, for how can one explain why the doe was there at exactly the right time and place? All I know is that in some incomprehensible way, the Universe had delivered.

A New Language for the Earth

A colleague of mine who works closely with the Nature devas, and leads school children and adults on his hugely popular day-long "walkabouts," shared this story that was related to him by a mother about some observations made by her three-year-old daughter. I think you'll agree that this little one is one of those special children that are here to teach us; one of those who have come in without a veil. The little girl said to her mother:

"Mommy, there's a new language that the Earth is speaking. The animals are talking to us; the trees are talking to us; the birds are talking, and the flowers are talking to us."

"But mommy," she continued, great concern in her voice, "nobody is listening!"

Today we have to remember how we once were able to listen to the Voices of Creation. They have much to teach us. The time has come when we can no longer turn a deaf ear to these Voices. Perhaps in the past we had a choice. But with our world rapidly spiraling toward destruction as a result of our disconnection with all Life on Earth, we no longer have a choice. We must make the leap from our long-held consciousness of separation to a new "unity consciousness." Separation is an illusion. Originally it was an illusion we embraced for the development of our individuality and with it the analytical mind. But somewhere along the way we forgot that it was an illusion, and we began acting as if it were real. When that happened, we experienced loneliness for the first time. In time out of this was born the idea of "us against them" – the belief that there were enemies. As I write these words I am suddenly flashing on a heart-wrenching encounter with an elk spirit that occurred while I drove over a low mountain pass in northern Idaho.

The elk's sudden presence in my automobile could not have been more palpable if it was physically present, and I had to pull off the road. "Please, it begged, try to stop their rapid development in so many of our mountain valleys. Since the beginning of our sojourn in this land, these [valleys] have been our winter refuges where we could be protected from the winter snows. Now in many places we are being forced to remain in the higher elevations where we have no protection from the winter snows." I was so overcome with its grief that I burst into uncontrollable tears.

Further back than we can remember, there has been a rift between the human and animal worlds. This has caused great suffering on both sides. Many of our species are being greatly stressed as a result of our disconnection from Life. Throughout the ages the animals have given much to us, and we owe much to them. It would be well to ponder this truth, not with your egoic mind but with a deep intuitive knowing. Whenever a single species dies out, something within each one of us dies as well. When a single life form is lost, we are the less. This is because our Life is One. Separation is an illusion. We all are part of a single unified field that some have called "God."

Learning to Read the Invisible Landscape

Part of the shift we must make is learning to read the invisible landscapes around us. A couple of years ago I was teaching at a retreat center in the mountains of southern Virginia. At one point in addressing the group, I raised the question of what the land had taught them since arriving. I asked if they were aware of the doe that came each morning around dawn to the northeast corner of the grassy area where we had our lunch. I continued:

"Besides the doe and her family, I've been aware of a pair of red-tail hawks that have a nest in a tall pine not too far from here. And has anyone become aware of the red-tail fox that has a burrow under the barn? She has just given birth to several kits, and she is a proud mother. Also, there's a six-foot pilot black snake that lives in the walls of the barn, and sometimes when you are there, you might hear a sudden thump. That's him dropping on his prey, which would most likely be a juicy field mouse. This species, like our bull snakes, is a member of the constrictor family which wrap around their victims, squeezing them to death. He's done a great job in keeping down the rodent population. And these snakes are often sought by farmers who recognize their value in maintaining a balance." I went on and mentioned a burrowing animal that lived under the wood shed.

At this point the owner and director of the retreat center stood up and proceeded to confirm everything I had said. And while what I had just done was inconceivable to some of those present, others began to be aware that they too had been getting similar impressions since having arrived. I reminded them that all of us have this ability, and my purpose was not to awe anyone but to demonstrate an ability that is within all of us.

Chapter 4 : Exposing the False Beliefs that Bind Us

A Web of Illusions

In my vision of Earth as a prison camp without walls, I saw that the vast majority of our world in every age, as far back as we began recording history, had been caught in a vast "web" of illusions about who we really are and the nature of our world itself. In many instances, to my great astonishment, it was a case of deliberate deceit. The interconnecting threads that formed the illusion were the beliefs of the times – beliefs that were not supported by any Truth or based on what is real.

In fact, I was shown that "belief" itself separates us from what is real. Remember what the East Indian master, Maharshi, said to the Harvard professors, Richard Alpert and Timothy Leary, who had been extolling the virtues of the transcendental experiences of LSD: "Better to become the Christ than to see him." He then, before their unbelieving eyes, proceeded to take a mega-dose of their drug with no visible effect.

Because most had become entrapped in the tyranny of the mind, these false beliefs had enormous power over the masses. Deep down, we all know what is true and real. It is ingrained. And that will be one of the great rediscoveries of the New Cycle we are poised now to enter.

Once we have become separated from our feeling nature, it is relatively easy for the vast majority of people to become controlled by a false belief system. These beliefs tend to be fundamentalist in nature, both secular and religious, and tend to evoke highly charged emotional reactions and a dogmatic approach. This tends to cloud the thinking process, eventually resulting in a closed mind.

Those people in every age, who chose to speak out, or to live a quiet, secluded life of freedom, have often been hunted down, imprisoned and put to death.

With this web of illusion a great fear settled over the masses. Fear is possible only when one is identified with the tyranny of the mind.

The "place of no fear" is the place of the high heart, which knows only unity and oneness.

Sadly, for centuries in the West the medieval Christian Church became the perfect vehicle for enforcing these false beliefs. Thus, the inquisitions, crusades, heresy trials, witch hunts, book burnings and systematic destruction of great libraries.

Even in other ancient cultures like the Egyptian and Aztec, it was a corrupt priesthood that ushered in dark periods of human sacrifice, dark rituals and a small elite taking control of the wealth, the power and the knowledge. A militant fundamentalist Christian Church served this role in the West, and a militant fundamentalist Islamic faith served that role in the Near East.

It was this web of illusion, based on false beliefs that formed this almost impenetrable ceiling over the Earth, preventing all but the strongest and most advanced to break through.

Let us look at the very big picture of what is going on today: Why have we been told that we are alone in the Universe, or that we are not being visited by advanced civilizations? Why have we been told that we are the first technologically advanced civilization? Who gains from these lies and deceptions? How does this serve an economic, political and especially religious elite?

Why have we been told that we are the pinnacle of evolution and that there's nothing beyond? I ask this: If we are the highest, then what hope is there?

Why do so many believe we are here for the first time, and that there is no evidence we survive bodily death, even though there is overwhelming evidence to the contrary? What do the most powerful and wealthiest religious institutions gain from this fabrication? How do they stand to benefit from our ignorance?

Deliverance

I have seen that beyond the above deception and rampant ignorance, there is great hope today. This is central to my message. I can tell you this: Know that our prayers for deliverance have been heard, and help is at hand, as it is for the aboriginal people all over the world whose cultures are threatened by extinction.

Not just our human prayers, but also those of other species have been heard. The great whales and dolphins, and the mighty elephants, being hunted to extinction, have also asked for help, as have the polar bears and the grandmother trees, all of whom are being decimated.

This consists of a great multi-species "calling," and that calling redounds to the farthest reaches of Creation. And help has been forthcoming, for how could it be otherwise? Our Infinite Creation is a Single Being who is totally aware of the whole, as well as the minutest part.

When your toe is infected, your whole body responds by sending forth antibodies or cells to destroy the infection. Your body is designed to take care of the individual parts because it knows it is one organism, and it is only as healthy as its weakest part. That is why great help and compassion will be coming forth from every corner of the Universe in response to our multi-species calling. We are never alone in our struggles.

False Beliefs of Our Time

Listed below are some of the false beliefs that I have recognized that have kept us from realizing our full potential. More will come to mind as our eyes begin to open, and we begin changing the way we perceive the world and our relationship with the world. Some beliefs are more deeply ingrained than others and cannot be simply contradicted. The mind might accept the changes, but the rest of you cannot.

A Formula for Neutralizing False Beliefs

Here is the threefold formula for neutralizing a false belief. Let us take for example the belief so widespread in our culture of "lack" or "not enough." There is not enough money, not enough time or not enough love, etc. Most of us cannot just affirm that we no longer believe in lack because the idea is so deeply engraved in our unconscious. So you will want to first (1) affirm the higher truth that there is abundance. In fact, you <u>are</u> abundance. It is not something you get. It is what you are. Second (2) is visualization or imaging. Form the image of a life of abundance and with abundance flowing to you from multiple sources. Three (3) is the correct feeling. As best you can, hold the feeling in your heart of what this abundance feels like. Imagine the joy it brings to you – the peace of mind.

Thus we have the threefold formula of: (1) the higher truth which can override the limiting belief, (2) the visualization: imaging will neutralize that false belief, and finally (3) the positive feeling which will magnetically attract to us you your heart's desire.

The "Keys" that are given in chapter eleven are a means of becoming free of these false beliefs. **But the keys must be felt, not thought about.** We will have to shift from the head to the heart space to image a "new you" that has come to perceive the world differently. The mind has no power to neutralize these false beliefs; it is not a soul function as is the higher feeling nature.

Place your hand over your heart to be sure you are in your heart. **I have discovered that many of us who are more cerebral are "thinking" about the heart rather than "being" in the heart.** Creating overtones through voice, didgeridoo or Tibetan bowls are effective means of shifting into the high heart.

You will know when you have made the shift because you will be centered in the present moment. This is the place of no fear. If you are analyzing the technique or "thinking about" belief systems, for example, you are still in your head. Identifying with the mind creates separation, and separation leads to fear. In the unity of the high heart, separation and fear are impossible.

Some Common False Beliefs

Limited Beings

Central to the false belief system that has kept our species in the state of disempowerment is the idea that we are limited beings. The ramifications of this concept serve to keep us as good, "worker bee" slaves to do the will of the controlling elite. I have already spoken about the fact that through a series of lucid dreams and visions, I became aware that the Earth is a prison camp, and that we have been trapped in this prison without walls. I pointed out that it is a prison of false belief systems that have become part of our consensus reality as a result of the efforts of the controlling elite. These false belief systems can be divided into two categories: one is the religious camp and the other is the secular camp, although some of these beliefs fall into both camps.

Religious Elite: A Chosen People

First is the idea that there is a religious elite, a chosen people, an elect, a God's people. This concept is not only elitist, but also separatist and divisive as elitism always is. Our Creator God does not favor a particular group of people or individuals. Our Creator chooses **all of us**. But **only a few** individuals or groups **respond to God's call and choose God**. The Jewish people were chosen, not because God favored them and chose them only, but because they chose God. Under Moses they sought to become a people of God.

Original Sin

I wish now to address the concept of what has been called Original Sin. This is perhaps one of the greatest hoaxes perpetrated on a large portion of humanity in the history of the world. Even after my ten years involvement with the institutional church, I still do not know what Original Sin is. It seems to say that a long time ago someone offended God, and as a result all of us are cursed, even though we were not involved in the original transgression. Even worse, the concept implies there is no hope for any of us to get out from under this curse by ourselves. We are told that we need outside help, that this outside help is only available through the mediation of the acceptable religion or religious authority, and only for the "true believers."

Salvation

Closely related to the doctrine of original sin is the idea of salvation, the idea that we need to be saved. Saved from what? Are we saved from the finality of death? We know now that death is not final. Everyone survives death, regardless of their beliefs, or even whether or not they believe in God. The idea that one needs salvation keeps organized religion in business as a self-perpetuating institution. It gives the ecclesiastical hierarchy great power, and has been a very effective tool of the ruling religious elite.

Divinity of Christ

The idea of the divinity of Christ has permeated Christianity. This concept separates us from everything to do with the life of Christ. If Christ was a God and not a human being, then what he did has little to do with our lives. The doctrine that Jesus is God or the only son of God has been knowingly used as a device to have power over the masses. Centuries ago **Pope Leo X said to his fellow bishops and cardinals: "The myth of Christ's divinity has served us well."** Such a statement is an admission that this is a myth, created by those in power for the purposes of power and control over others.

Myth of the Second Coming

The idea that Jesus himself will come again is another myth perpetrated on the masses. It goes like this: "Christ came; his

88

mission was aborted; he will come again!" This keeps us paying our tithes and waiting for a deity to come and set things right, rather than living a Christ-like life ourselves. For the Jewish Messiah, it is a little different, but the end result is the same: "Jesus of Nazareth came; he was not the One; we wait for another!" And, of course, while we are waiting, we can support our local synagogue.

Life Is a Struggle

Another belief in the religious camp that has become part of the secular camp is the Protestant work ethic that life must be a struggle. According to this ethic we must work hard every day. If we struggle and work hard, we may have enough food to eat and the bare necessities of life. The key word here is struggle. The false belief is that we are condemned to struggle here on Earth. In the Creation story man must "work by the sweat of his brow." This very belief creates struggle. When effort becomes struggle, then we are going in the wrong direction. This false belief system insists **that each person must EARN the right to life, liberty and the pursuit of happiness**. This suggests that these are not inalienable rights, but must be earned. If we do not work hard enough, then we do not deserve life, liberty or the pursuit of happiness. Instead we deserve to suffer. And unfortunately this is the thinking of many people.

"Subdue the Earth"

Of all the false belief systems that have been part of the consensus reality, one of the most terrible is found in the opening chapters of Genesis, where God tells man to "subdue the Earth and have dominion over all the creatures of the Earth." This concept was inserted later as a result of the patriarchal takeover of the Church. This one verse alone has been used as justification for greed and exploitation of our magnificent Earth. The idea is that the Earth belongs to us rather than our belonging to the Earth. It suggests that the Earth is something we can own and divide up and parcel out. We can buy and sell it as we please. It is this false belief system that has brought us to the brink of destruction. It has led to the environmental crisis and put us on a self-destructive course. The threat is not only to human life, but to all life on the planet. Even the phrases that we use suggest an aggressive and hostile attitude toward our Earth and all Nature. In our school books, we learned about our "conquest of Nature." We heard about the "taming of the frontier" and were told that a hostile wilderness needed to be tamed. There is little that is gentler, more loving or more nurturing than Nature.

The idea of subduing the Earth and having dominion over all life as a mandate God gives to his human creatures is a false philosophy. Man has a way of attributing to God what serves his own agendas. This is the agenda that serves certain human beings for justifying greed and exploitation of our Earth and our natural resources. All this has led to environmental collapse.

Guilt

Another false belief is that of guilt. The very idea of guilt causes people to be tormented, to make terrible judgments on themselves and others. Guilt is not a natural emotion or a natural part of who we are.

There is a true story of a time when the Jesuits came to an island in the Caribbean. So happy and contented were the native people that the priests were unable to convert them into good Catholics. The natives had no concept of sin and saw no reason to repent or be saved. So the Jesuits had a problem, which they solved by translating the Scriptures into the native language in a way that depicted these people as the ones who killed Christ. This insidious misrepresentation devastated the native people. It did not take long before they were converted into good Catholics, because they realized they needed "to be saved."

We Are Without Soul Powers

A religious misconception that I talk about a lot, is that the powers attributed to Christ, Moses and Saint Francis are the exclusive domain of only a few great souls who lived mostly in the remote past. I return repeatedly to this one idea that has become part of our consensus reality, because it is one of the major false beliefs that has been perpetrated in our culture and prevented us from awakening our soul powers.

God Judges

Another big one on the religious front is that God judges. Suffice it to say, our Creator God does not judge, nor does she punish. She creates! She has given us an infinite Universe that is governed by certain laws. When we live outside these laws, we experience neither judgment nor punishment, but consequence. There is no one out there judging us. When we put our finger in the fire, we get burned. That is not God's judgment; it is a consequence of trying to live outside the law.

God Punishes

Another false belief is that God punishes. I have said that if we should go through a major environmental collapse, then those of the conservative religious camp will blame it on God's punishment, and the more secular ones will say that Nature has failed us. Neither will be true! The truth will be that what is happening environmentally, and the suffering brought on by this is the result of the human species attempting to live outside the laws of Creation, and becoming a law unto themselves. When we put our finger in the fire and get burned, it is consequence, not God's punishment.

We Should Be "Truth Seekers"

A more subtle false belief in the more liberated spiritual camp is the concept of a "truth seeker." This sounds good and right, but it is very seductive. When we are continually seeking something, there is the implicit idea that Truth is outside of ourselves. All Truth is within. It is not something apart from us, because we are the Truth. We are love. We are wisdom. The idea of being a truth seeker suggests that we must continually seek. There are some who seek and seek all of their lives, but never find. Better than being a truth seeker is to know the Truth, to be a carrier of the Truth, and to be a living embodiment of the Truth.

Need for Security

In the secular camp, one of the false beliefs is that we need security. For ages politicians have known that people will respond to a perceived or real threat by giving away their freedom in exchange for security. This is what we did recently after 9/11 with the perceived threat of terrorism. We gave up many of our Constitutional Rights by passing the Patriot Act. This method has been used by the ruling elite for centuries to get control over the masses. A real or perceived threat is created and security is offered, but offered at a price – often the price being the loss of many freedoms.

Our perceived need for security has led to the "fear-based, survival mentality of our time." We fear we may not have enough food. We fear that we may not be able to pay the bills or the mortgage; we fear we may not be able to hold down a job. We only have to watch the ads on television to be indoctrinated with fears that something terrible might happen to us. Our house may burn down; we might be in a terrible accident. We might lose everything. There are big fears and small fears. The idea of a fear-based society creates anxiety among most people. Ask yourself who benefits from this distortion of the Truth. I suspect you will not have to look far.

The Need for Doctors and Medications

Another false belief is that when we are sick, we need to see a doctor or get medication. How often have we given up our power to doctors and the pharmaceuticals? We have lost the whole idea of being able to take care of ourselves and only going to a doctor under extreme circumstances. Now when we get sick, we think we need a prescription. This is almost automatic for many in our culture. The message is that we are powerless. This has created a great dependence on pharmaceuticals and doctors in our country and around the world.

The Myth of Freedom

One of the biggest deceptions placed on the American people is the idea that we are free. The United States especially has indoctrinated us with the idea that we are a free nation and a free people. It is found in our history books; we have grown up with it. The idea that perhaps we are not free and do not live in a free country is shocking to most people. They will argue vehemently against this idea. The realization that we are not really free is the beginning of our freedom.

The Myth of Acceptable Appearance

Another false belief is the idea of how we should look. For example, women today are indoctrinated with the idea that they should be thin. This idea is perpetuated by the fashion industry and a coterie of feminine men, who apparently prefer women to look more like adolescent boys. We need to ask ourselves why this is the only culture in the world that has had women looking like scarecrows as the ideal woman. Renaissance women and women of any culture or any age were feminine and full-bodied. In other cultures being full-bodied was a virtue; in our culture it is anathema.

Who is it that benefits from this industry? We do not have to look far to see the multibillion-dollar diet and fitness industries, not to mention the fashion industries that benefit greatly from this. We have to ask ourselves what this does to many women. Most women cannot look like the modern ideal. And if they did, it would be unhealthy. It creates a sense of not being beautiful and not liking one's body – or even hating one's body. A body might be beautiful by the standards of another culture. But by our culture very few women are able to meet that impossible standard. We usually do not have to look very far to find if there is greed and profit in this image.

The Myth of Dumb Animals

Another is the idea of dumb animals that lack souls, intelligence and consciousness, and are unable to communicate with us. If we accept this idea, it makes it easier to accept the practices of slaughtering animals for food or doing lab experiments on them. As long as we have this myth, people will not be upset by the plight of animals in this world.

The Belief of "Multiple Use" and "Managed" Wilderness

Our Forest Service has adopted the slogan of "multiple use forests," which I call "multiple abuse." Notice the words "multiple use" and "managed." The wilderness did pretty well without human beings managing it. Then we came to use land as we saw fit, and we destroyed much of the wilderness area. The idea that we own wilderness, that it is something to divide up and parcel out and do with as we please, is one of the terrible false beliefs that have gotten us into the environmental crisis that we are faced with at this time.

The Illusion of Separation

Another belief is that we are separated from the Earth; we are separated from God, and from one another. In the opening chapters of Genesis, we are "cast out from the garden." It is the idea of being separate from life, from Nature and from God. In reality it is impossible to be separate from God or from anything else in Creation. For that matter, the only time we experience the separation is when we buy into this false belief that we are separate. This idea is almost universal in our culture today.

The Myth of Lack

Another idea is that of lack: There is not enough money, not enough time, not enough food, not enough material things, not enough love. Some of us have been indoctrinated with this idea more than others. This belief of lack tends to create a life of lack, a life in which we truly do not have enough because we have accepted this is the way things are.

Survival of the Fittest

One of the most terrible beliefs that we have accepted is that of "survival of the fittest." This observation of Darwin is true only on the level of biological life. It does not apply to the level of conscious beings. This idea of survival of the fittest has been used by the controlling elite to give to the strong and take from the weak, because they say we do not know how to handle responsibility or money or power or knowledge. It has become a rationale. A higher ethic is that the strong lift up the weak, that the strong care for the weak, so that the weak have an opportunity to become strong.

The False Ethic of Competition

A related ethic is that of competition. This is very strong in our capitalist society. In a competitive society, there are not only winners, but losers. A more evolved society is not based on competition and survival of the fittest. If we are to survive as a species, we need to make the leap to a higher understanding of unity and oneness.

The Belief That We Need Laws

Another false belief is that we need laws for everything. A higher, more evolved society is one in which the government that governs least is the one that governs best. The most advanced civilizations we have had on this planet are those that had almost no laws. In these advanced societies it was understood that the Truth is that everyone and each individual instinctively knows what to do. The assumption in our modern world is that most people do not know what to do. This gives the controlling elite the right to make decisions for others.

The False Belief That We Are the Mind

I speak of this idea in other places; however, it is important to understand that much of the suffering we experience today is the result of identification with the mind. The mind reads duality and separation. When we try to create good, there is an inherent evil that is created along with the good. This idea is expressed in the Creation story of man eating of the fruit of the knowledge of good and evil. The meaning behind this is that we fell into duality at an earlier point in our history.

The Belief That We Need to Prepare for the Future

The above idea is pervasive in our society. When we are trapped in the illusion of linear time, then we fear that we may not be prepared for some future event or future catastrophe. Such fears pull us out of the present moment and disempower us. Think about all the times you have fretted about the future – at times with high anxiety. The vast majority of what we have feared did not happen, and what did happen obviously did not annihilate us. We are still here, aren't we? How much time and energy was wasted?

Our Response to the Controllers

How then should we respond to this? We are moving from a culture of separation to a culture of unity and oneness. Thus it is no longer appropriate to blame others, no matter what they may have done. Rather, we need to see that they, the "Controllers," are a part of us, they reflect us, and they are us. We can even have a certain appreciation for our enemies, because they make us stronger and help us to see where we are weak. A chain is only as strong as its weakest link. Therefore, we need our enemies, but we do not have to capitulate or roll over and belly up. We must use the resistance from the controlling elite as a means to move forward and to accelerate our growth.

An automobile that has tires spinning on ice cannot go forward because there is no resistance. We need a certain amount of resistance to accelerate. Some would say that we are faced with overwhelming resistance, but then let us respond with overwhelming strength and determination. Quite possibly the threat of extinction and the pressure of a controlling elite that would enslave us provide the perfect evolutionary pressure for us to make the necessary shift. **I am speaking of the shift from the tyranny of the mind to the embrace of the high heart, the shift from thinking to feeling.** For in so doing, we will create a paradise on Earth. We will create a New Eden.

We are beings with limitless power at our disposal. If we could know the totality of what we are and who we are, we would never question our ability. A number of stories in my earlier book, Soul on Fire, show how a few people can bring about enormous change and do enormous good, against all odds. Sometimes a single person doing a sacred ceremony can affect not only people but the land around them. I told the story of the woman who did a ceremony at the Grand Canyon which apparently prevented quakes from happening in southern California. Everything is related, everything is part of a vast unified field.

Our Response to the Ceiling

What is our response to those who have attempted to enslave and control the majority of our species? Do we feel the need to find a light saber and do battle with the bad guys? I certainly hope not because it has been tried many times and never very successfully. Do not waste your energies opposing your oppressors – it only makes them stronger. Furthermore, it would compromise our purpose for being here. "Resist not evil," it has been said. It is because by resisting, we empower our enemy, and we are drawn into the negativity so that it can infect us. The *I Ching* says: "When negativity comes forth, it is a wise person that withdraws."

We have heard it said that we become what we love. There is a Hindu maxim that says you "become what you hate." Both are true. I would like to add to those by saying that we become what we do battle against. We become what we continually resist. Therefore, do not go to battle against negativity. **The** Earth's vernacular at this time is very much about doing battle. Remember what happened when prohibition laws were passed to do away with the evils of alcohol. It was prohibition that gave a foothold for the first time for organized crime to come into this country. This is quite often the way. Therefore, instead of doing battle, begin exposing the lies and secrets of the ruling elite.

We begin by knowing and speaking the truth, living the truth and realizing the truth within our own life, by making our life a living embodiment of the truth, by being a carrier of the truth itself. Expose the false belief systems of our time, demonstrate to others how they too can be free. This is why you are here. This is why we have committed to coming to the Earth at this time: to be a carrier of positivity. This is the very purpose you have come in for. Be the embodiment of compassion and joy, inner quiet, inner harmony, balance and courage. Our example will inspire and give permission for others to do likewise.

The oppressors, the controlling elite, are not my enemies. I do not personally support what they do, but my enemy is within, as it is with all of us. We are our own enemy when we acquiesce, when we look in the other direction, in hopes that it will go away.

It is true that we have been misinformed and misled, sometimes in almost diabolical ways. But each one of us is still completely and totally responsible for the way things are. We are totally responsible for allowing ourselves to be misled. It has been said that the greatest error in the Tao is to not accept responsibility for what happens to us or for the way things are. As we begin to accept responsibility for our situation, it is the beginning of our liberation. We are moving from a culture of separation to one of unity and oneness. It is never useful to point the finger or blame others, no matter what they have done.

I was told that as these ideas became accepted more and more, a growing number of people would begin to spontaneously experience an awakening of such powers, just as I experienced these with an amazing spontaneity. The personal trigger for me was when I made the decision to test the promise of a first-century Hebrew Master: "These things and more shall you be able to do!" And so I ask each of you, my readers, "are you too willing to claim that promise?" Are you willing to make it **your truth** as I did for myself? It seems that from the beginning I was put to the test. And yet it was as if I could not fail. It was as if the script had been already written out for me. In fact, it seemed that the script had been written out before I came into this life. We do not really understand time, but time is not what we think it is. Time runs both ways, and in a certain sense the future has already happened.

It took time for me to figure out how to teach these concepts. I knew that it was not just some magic pill that people could take to awaken these abilities. I began to realize it is not so much what we do, but what we need to stop doing that is blocking us from awakening our true nature. We need to begin by letting go of the beliefs in which we have been indoctrinated since we were toddlers. Then we need to stop doing the things that separate us from our true self.

Chapter 5: Attitudes and Practices That Keep Us in Bondage

Attitudes that Keep Us in Bondage:

I want to talk about the attitudes that keep us in bondage. It is not so much what we need to do; it is simply that we need to stop doing the things that we do. These are the things that bar our return to Edenic consciousness.

The Loop of Judgments

There is a loop of judgments that few people understand. When we judge another person, we are judging ourselves because there is only One Being, and we are all a part of the unified field of that Great Oneness. Thus we have a saying, "Judge not that ye be not judged." It is not a moral issue but a matter of quantum physics. It is how the world and the universe work. Judgment of others always results in judgment of self.

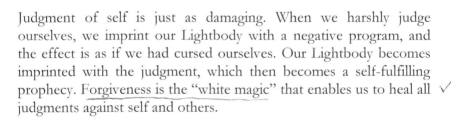

Judgment of self is just as damaging. When we harshly judge ourselves, we imprint our Lightbody with a negative program, and the effect is as if we had cursed ourselves. Our Lightbody becomes imprinted with the judgment, which then becomes a self-fulfilling prophecy. Forgiveness is the "white magic" that enables us to heal all judgments against self and others.

Obsession with Worry

The second attitude that can separate us from our soul path is worry. Most people are worrying constantly over many things. This tendency to obsess can be healed by turning your life over to a higher destiny. It also can be healed by simply not dwelling on the future and letting go of your control issues.

Control Issues

Worry comes from the feeling that we are not in control. In fact, we can say that control issues are yet a third attitude that can separate us from the Edenic consciousness. Control issues, then, are healed by surrender and letting go. Surrender is tied in with the powers of the Western direction. It is the Goddess of the West who teaches us to surrender and let go of all that is no longer life-giving and life-sustaining. We carry around far too much baggage. The Serpent Goddess will help us unload that burden.

The Chaos

Another attitude is what my partner and I affectionately call the "chaos grid." When we get caught up in the chaos grid, it separates us from our inner being, and we lose the power of the Void. We lose the power of the Primal Stillness from which everything arises. The chaos grid is not evil in itself, but it puts us in a state in which we are completely scattered. We are no longer focused on the present moment. It is very disempowering.

The Pathology of Fear

Another attitude that separates us is the pathology of fear. Fear can be overcome by the realization that Creation is one being. Fear is a pathology of our culture today. We are living in a fear-based society. We live in a survival mentality. This is how the negative forces maintain control of our culture, by keeping us in that survival mentality. Who benefits by our survival mentality? How do the media contribute to this survival mentality? When am I going to eat? Where am I going to live? Where is my next paycheck coming from? Will I hold onto my job? Fear paralyzes. It renders us incapable of acting with power in our lives.

Attitude of Self-Importance

Self-importance is not a function of our true self but of the ego's identification with the mind. When we are caught up in self-importance, we have lost the power of the Void. We have become separated from the Silence that has no opposite.

Self-importance is healed by the realization that nothing anyone can do or say can add to that which we are, or in any way diminish us. When we hold that thought, and it really sinks in, then we find that self-importance is resolved.

Obsession with Self-Absorption

Many people are caught up in the bubble of self-reflection and are looking at themselves, analyzing what they are going to do next or what they have just done. Self-absorption can be healed by service toward others. Service toward others will resolve the excessive focus on oneself.

The Fires of Our Anger

Many people carry a great deal of anger in our world today. Saint Germain has said that anger is "magic run amok." Anger is the downside of our passions, which are a manifestation of the fires of our soul. Anger can be healed by stepping into another's skin and becoming that person.

Obsession with Needing

When we realize that we are already complete, and that we simply have not actualized what we are, when we realize there is nothing outside of ourselves that we do not already have, then we can finally let go of needing. Needing is understood by the universe as a negative vibration that pushes things away, rather than attracting them. There is nothing that will block us from trying to manifest something in our life more than needing it too much in the sense that we cannot be happy or complete without it.

Practices That Separate Us from Our True Nature:

Tyranny of the Telephone

A common practice that separates us is what I call the "tyranny of the telephone." The advent of cell phones has increased the problem exponentially. Phones pull us away from the present moment. When we are continually on the phone, we are separated from the present moment. Obsession with our favorite toy – the computer – likewise separates us from direct experience.

The Cult of I-Me-Mine

Many people in our world today, especially in the West, are caught up in the cult of I-Me-Mine. This cult suggests that we are separated from the whole, that there are things that we need or possess. This is mine; this is for me! There is no love or truth in this attitude.

Obsession with Agendas

Many people today have to set agendas for everything. This creates a sense of disquiet when one is continually carrying around agendas, for how can we be content with that which is, which is a blissful state of being?

The Demon of Distractions

The demon of distractions is a big problem today. There has never been an age in which there were so many distractions. It sometimes takes heroic measures to let go of these distractions in life. We avoid being pulled into distractions by being present with self. Identification with those things that distract us makes it almost impossible to turn loose of them.

The Practice of Being Hurried

Being too hurried can be healed by becoming "time-rich." Becoming time-rich means that we recognize time as an illusion and we consciously use that illusion to serve us. We then discover that time becomes very pliable, capable of being expanded or greatly contracted. We become hurried when we feel there is not enough time.

Needing Results

Doing things for results is yet another practice that separates us. When we are preparing a meal, we should be chopping vegetables or adding seasoning for the joy of chopping vegetables or adding seasoning, not so that we can finish making dinner. This practice again takes us out of the present moment.

The Entrapment of Attachments

Another practice that separates us is that of attachments. We become attached to things in the physical world in our consumer culture. We become convinced that we need gadgets, that we need lots of things. Many of us may have evolved beyond this, but we also get attached on the next level, which is that of emotions and feelings. And finally, we can get attached to belief systems on the mental level. So there is a danger of attachment to the physical, emotional and mental. This tendency can be healed by letting go of these attachments on every level and just by being in the world but not of it!

Chapter 6: Our Conscious Creation

Our observation of the natural world can open us to the idea that we are a part of a *C*onscious Creation that is deeply aware of us – a Creation that not only instructs and nourishes us but reflects and adapts itself to us in the most profound sense of the word. Behind this wondrous Creation there are Great Beings that are deeply invested in our evolution and fulfillment.

It might be helpful for just a moment to try to forget all you have been told about our world because chances are it was wrong.

Our world is a magical world where things are not as they seem to our conscious mind. In fact our rational mind is incapable of comprehending this world of ours. In the last four decades I have experienced and witnessed much that is simply outside the syntax of our culture. It might be advisable not to try to fit the stories and concepts I am sharing with what you think you know.

Approach our wondrous world with a beginner's mind which is a childlike openness to everything you encounter. Allow every experience you have, every landscape you come across, every mountain, river, tree, tiny flower or insect to be as if you were experiencing it for the first time. In this regard I have been blessed to have an extraordinary teacher, my partner Astrid, who came into this world with the gift of an ecstatic connection to everything in Nature. When you can do these things, you will be well rewarded and you cannot help but be transformed.

I would like to give you some idea of how conscious animals are as well as the whole of Creation. Had someone suggested this idea to me four decades ago when I was an Episcopal priest, I would have said "no way!"

In my book *Soul on Fire*, I have told the story of how my partner and I warned a family of deer that grazed each afternoon across a meadow from our home outside of the town of Knoxville, Tennessee. At one point we encouraged them to begin grazing close to our home since hunting season had begun and we knew they would not be safe. We were already hearing gun shots. That evening they came to our porch steps with one of them calling to us in a peculiar bleating sound I had never heard before. The one that was calling to us was stretching her head toward our door as if she were trying to let us know she had received the message. Amazingly they continued to graze around our house throughout hunting season and were joined by other deer. At the end of hunting season we communicated to them that the danger was over, and the next day they were back grazing at their former habitat.

When we moved to Townsend, which borders Smoky Mountain National Park, my wife and I did a ceremony to bring back the panthers which had been hunted to extinction over a century ago in our area and had not been seen since. These "panthers," as they were called, were once native to the southern mountains and were believed by some to be a cross between the western cougar and the Florida black panther. We nearly fainted when six weeks later a large feline screamed no more than a hundred feet from us when we were in a wilderness area not far from our home. We knew without a doubt that its piercing scream, so unmistakable, was to let us know that our summons had been answered and they had indeed returned. Less than a year later a female panther actually appeared to several people, proudly showing off her three cubs.

Size is not a criterion for awareness in the animal kingdom. Not long ago I was in front of my home when my attention was directed to a moth crawling up the trunk of the tree I was leaning against. Feeling a connection with the tiny creature, I sent it love. To my surprise is stopped and arched its back much like a cat. Whenever I stopped sending the love vibration it would resume crawling up the trunk. Each time I sent love, the moth stopped and arched its back and then continued crawling as before. The third time it made a one-hundred-eighty degree turn, crawled down the trunk to my hand, then proceeded to crawl on top of my hand and remain there.

I was engaged in the universal mode of communication recognizable in every part of our infinite universe. That mode of course is love combined with imaging.

One of the first times my apprentices tried this means of communication was when a carload of them was leaving our base camp in the red rock canyon country of central Utah where I had taken a group of students for a sacred wilderness journey. When they had driven no more than a half mile on the Forest Service road, a coyote crossed the road in front of the car, and continued running off across the prairie. Anxious to test the ideas I had been teaching them, they stopped the car and began to send love to the coyote along with the invitation that it come back to visit them. At the exact moment they sent the message, the coyote, now a hundred feet away, stopped and turned to begin walking back to the automobile. It slowly circled the car a couple of times, then rolled over in front the car, showing its belly like a dog showing its vulnerability. All this time the coyote was looking back at the group in the car. The apprentices at that moment got their first taste of the ecstasy of being in direct communication with another being we share this world with.

Here is another example of our Conscious Creation; it is my favorite dolphin story. A friend of ours in a most unusual way was given a series of sounds which she was told would call the dolphins to her. Several months later she and her daughter were at the beach together. It was late afternoon and the other bathers had left. They were standing in about three feet of water when suddenly they noticed they had been encircled by a school of sharks. With their escape to shore blocked, my friend was in a state of near panic when her twenty-two year old daughter, accompanying her, said, "Mom, we should call in the dolphins with the sounds that were given to you!" With no other recourse they started vocalizing the complex sounds she had been given only weeks earlier. Seconds later, as she described, "the biggest dolphin we had ever seen jumped over the circle of sharks and swam next to us. And the sharks were out of there in seconds."

Another story I love about animal protectors was shared by a young man of about twenty-six. He explained to me that as far back as he could remember he had had experiences in which hawks had been responsible for saving his life. On one such occasion while he was driving up a winding mountain road, a pair of red tail hawks began dive-bombing his automobile and brushing against the windshield. So obstructed was his vision that he was forced off the road onto the shoulder. No sooner had he turned onto the shoulder than an eighteen wheeler appeared barreling down around the curb ahead of him on his side of the road. After recovering from his shock, he realized that the hawks had just saved his life.

On another occasion while he and his dad were fishing in a small boat several miles out in the ocean, a pair of hawks started circling over head. He said to his father, "Dad we have got to get to shore, there is going to be a storm." His dad argued that the sky was clear and there had been no storms predicted. However, so insistent was he that his dad reluctantly headed for shore. And it was just in time! It turned out that a sudden storm did rapidly blow in and they barely made it.

Some Comments about Sacred Ceremonies

I have spoken often of the importance of sacred ceremonies for commanding the elements and for healing the Earth, our animal friends and fellow humans. I have pointed out that this is a way of awakening our primal power and shifting to the "second attention" that certain Native American tribes speak of. The second attention is our awareness of the inner world and the inner senses.

Once these connections have been made, however, ceremonies largely become unnecessary much of the time. At this point, as both Astrid and I have demonstrated on a number of occasions, intention and the spoken word are all that is required. We have simply "summoned" the powers or called them forth into manifestation. There is also the occurrence of calling forth from higher levels of consciousness what is desired or needed. This, then, often is accomplished without the spoken word and is an ability found in the more advanced Initiates.

Never forget that power is not something outside of us. We are power! We are simply calling power into manifestation.

Of course, from another equally accurate perspective, there is a type of "outside" power. I am speaking especially of the elemental powers and beings that abide in the energetic world. Every shaman worth his salt knows this and realizes the importance of accessing help from this realm. The reality of all of this is that the outer and the inner are really part of the same reality.

In other writings I have said that the energetic universe is far more ancient, vaster and more complex than our physical universe. This energetic world is our primary reality, but we have forgotten this truth.

In the New Earth that is rapidly being ushered in, this energetic world will begin to make itself known, to reveal itself to our senses so that in a relatively short time it will become visible again as it was in ancient times. The above is already happening with the more awakened of our species, but soon many others will follow. Our human species will become surprised to discover that we are not alone in this world, and that we share this Earth with a host of other sentient beings without whom we would be unable to survive.

Chapter 7: Awakening the *Siddhis*

My Experience of Awakening the *Siddhis*

In the Foreword of this book I have stated that in both Native and African traditions it is said that each of us come here with a purpose that we alone can fulfill. The problem is that we forget what that purpose is and spend years trying to remember what we are supposed to do. I was fortunate that, in a vision I had in 1971, while I was still a priest in the Episcopal Church, I was shown what my purpose was. I was told that in previous lifetimes I had awakened my soul powers and become liberated, but in this life I had chosen to forget who I was and experience the ecstasy of awakening them once more. Not only was I to awaken these spiritual powers or *siddhis* as they are called in Vedic tradition, but to demonstrate them as abilities that are latent in all humans. I was also to remember my past lives here on Earth and to understand the lessons of these previous lives. The next part of the message stunned me. I was told I had to achieve these things without the benefit of a teacher, and in fact I would have no teacher in this lifetime.

I have said that the reason for the above was that, whereas in each generation, on the average, only a few dozen people awakened in our world, in the New Cycle there would eventually be millions awakening and there would not be enough teachers to go around.

My task therefore was to show that this awakening can be achieved through a direct relationship with the Creation without benefit of a teacher, guru, master, ashram or mystery school as had always been the case in the past.

In spite of my apprehension during the next several decades, these soul memories and powers surfaced almost effortlessly. In time, as foretold in my vision, I found myself demonstrating them before numerous individuals and groups.

Had I been brought up in an East Indian culture, what was happening to me would have been recognized, but without a tradition to fall back on, I simply had to go on instinct.

What I did not realize for a number of years is that I seemed to be the only non-indigenous person in the West that had actually experienced a full awakening of the *siddhis* and has been willing to speak openly about it. I will therefore describe my experience of awakening and demonstrating some of the powers that surfaced in me.

During the 70s when Yuri Geller was appearing on numerous television talk shows demonstrating his ability to bend spoons, he was creating quite a sensation. But when a Native shaman was told about this amazing "white man," he said, somewhat curiously: "That's interesting but what else can he do?"

As far as I know his promoter replied, "That's all!"

"You mean to tell me that he can do only one thing?" the Native shaman replied, wondering what all the sensation was about.

This story shows how little our culture understands about the spiritual powers that are available to us. As far as spoon bending goes, I have never tried it but several of my apprentices have and were able to do it the first time. Attempting to duplicate Geller's spoon bending was of little interest to our group who had witnessed, and were beginning to develop much more impressive abilities that might have some practical value as well.

Another area of ignorance that I find so widespread among those in the West that are on spiritual paths are that spiritual powers are found only in teachers with red, yellow or copper skin. This, of course, is a type of reverse prejudice, but it certainly is a disempowering concept to many people who are not of color. Hopefully I have been able to refute that myth.

Over a period of three decades I conducted more than sixty ceremonies to end drought or excessive rain with about ninety-five percent success. Always the storms began to arrive within twenty-four hours and nearly all of them were unexpected. Sometimes the media would report that the storm would "materialize out of nowhere". There were also occasions where for the sake of demonstration before a group, I was able to call in thunder storms within the hour.

A few of these ceremonies were carried out from across the country. I soon realized that when it comes to influencing any of these primal forces of creation, distance is not a factor. Using intention I was able to materialize, or spilt the storm in half or dissipate it.

One weekend when Astrid and I were to teach an outdoor class on Shamanism, we were faced with the prediction of torrential rain throughout the weekend. Our answer to that was to call in the *Four-Direction Winds,* which kept the storm clouds at bay throughout the weekend. It was an amazing phenomenon to watch, for whenever the rain clouds would roll in, a wind would materialize from the opposite direction to push them back. Then when the tenacious storm tried to come in from another direction, a wind would arrive to counter that. Even with the storm raging around us, we kept dry for the entire weekend. Admittedly this incredible interplay of wind, water and sunshine put on quite a show that out-classed the subject matter of our program. Of course we all understood that the real teaching for that weekend came from the elements themselves, and sometimes I would just stop in mid-sentence so we could all watch and observe this drama of Creation.

There are humorous episodes connected with each element. I quickly learned that each elemental power has a marvelous sense of humor and perhaps this was designed to keep us from taking ourselves too seriously and to lighten up.

Once with a group of twenty people gathered under a clear blue sky in western Wyoming, I called for rain, and at the close of the ceremony we experienced thirty seconds of rain overhead. To our astonishment the only place in the state that got rain that day was a hundred foot diameter were our group was standing. Everywhere else it was dry as a bone.

Once on the River of No Return Wilderness in Northern Idaho, where I had taken a group of adults on their first vision quest, I called in too much wind and had to exhort the sometimes overly enthusiastic Wind devas to cease and desist after a number of tents where blown away and the blankets covering our sweat lodge were sent flying.

Another time while preparing for a sweat lodge with a group, I had to point out to them that the willow saplings they had used to construct the sweat lodge dome where too thin and not sturdy enough. As I was pointing this out, a dust devil that had formed on the hillside several hundred feet from where we were standing began dancing back and forth and then making a beeline for our sweat lodge. On some level I knew what was about to happen. Perhaps without consciously realizing it, I had requested that our group have this marvelous lesson. At any rate the dust devil exploded our fire, scattering the sticks and coals in a thirty-foot radius and totally flattening the sweat lodge. Everyone stared unbelievably. How could this have happened? And what did it mean? Then, as if on cue, all got it at the same time and burst into riotous laughter from the teaching they had just been given by the Primal Forces of Creation. It was a lesson they would never forget. The next day featured possibly the sturdiest sweat lodge I had ever seen.

I would say that the Fire elementals are perhaps peerless in the humorous scenarios they can manifest for our learning. In my early book, *Soul on Fire,* I described the assistance I received in helping a high school senior I had been counseling to break his drug addiction. I described my decision following a counseling session with him to request that the Fire spirits build a fire "under his ass." What I did not realize was that they took my directive literally, and five minutes later the crotch of his pants burst into flames. He was not a smoker so there were no matches or lighters on his person. Another story I described was a pyrotechnic display that was a result of a lesson I wished to give to someone who was psychically attacking several of my apprentices.

Astrid twice witnessed this command over the Fire element shortly after we were married. The first time it happened was one evening with a stack of fliers for a workshop I was scheduled to teach at a healing center in our area. We were questioning the wisdom of teaching there because of some negativity we had encountered with a sponsoring group. At that moment, to our astonishment, the fliers burst into flames. We had our answer and changed the location of the workshop. As a result the workshop was very well attended, whereas before changing to a new location it had received only a few applicants.

During this same time period we received a phone call from a woman who had developed psychic problems after working with a Ouija board. It was obvious to us that she had become overshadowed by a malevolent spirit intent on doing her and others harm. We agreed to help and set up a date to get together. However, after we had hung up the phone, a candle on an end table next to our bed suddenly exploded and set on fire a cloth doily.

At first Astrid, having had no experience of such things, was alarmed. But I assured her it was only our friends, the Fire elementals, doing their job. The spirit possessing the woman, alarmed at our intervention, quickly aborted its intention to attack us after it had gotten "burned."

Our vision quests and wilderness journeys provided wonderful settings and opportunity for demonstrations. Astrid and I loved to announce that one of us had called in a storm and watch our students scurry for their tents when without warning the thunder exploded overhead, and the storm actually materialized where we were camping. On one of these occasions after materializing a storm I promised to have the storm spirits join us in our sweat lodge that evening. When we opened the doors to the West, which is the natural home of the *Thunder Beings,* to the astonishment of our participants we began hearing rolling thunder that lasted for the next twenty minutes. It ended abruptly when we closed the sweat lodge door and reopened it to honor the powers of the North. Once again these amazing Beings cooperated perfectly by speaking to us at the time I had designated, enabling me to keep my promise.

I recall another vision quest at the Red Rock country of Utah, when Astrid and I called in a thunderstorm to get water running again in a stream bed that was nearly dry as a result of prolonged drought. When the storm materialized overhead several hours later, a participant remarked that "You and Astrid do not just talk about these things, you do them." He had never seen anything like it and returned home at the end of that week with an expanded view of our world and the possibilities in all of us.

It was at this time of Awakening that I began to be aware of a growing sense of elation that ultimately erupted into ecstatic joy that is almost indescribable. That elation was the result of conscious unity I was experiencing with the whole of Creation. I had let go of much of my human-based consciousness. This is our true path as humans in this world – to achieve a conscious union with All That Is.

In Control of One's Power

It was during the early stages of the awakening of my spiritual powers that I learned some important lessons I will never forget. It was that one must be in control of whatever powers or energies one invokes. To be able to call in such powers does not mean that one should. When Robert Oppenheimer figured out how to make the first H-bomb it did not mean that he was correct in doing so. It was a moral issue that tormented him and he struggled with the rest of his life.

When Alexandra David-Neel, the first western woman to become a Tibetan Lama, decided to see if she could use her mind power to create an artificial Being called a *Tulka,* she was amazed at her success. The energetic Being, which resembled a monk, accompanied her, like a faithful servant, wherever she went. When it began to get out of control, she went to her teacher, who was the abbot that had trained her. When she explained her problem, asking for his help, he refused, saying: "Whatever you created, you must be able to de-create." Alexandra then had to spend a number of tension-filled days before she was successful in dissolving this creature that was becoming more and more threatening to her.

In the story I related earlier about Astrid's successful attempt to still a thirty-five mile per hour wind that had been blowing continuously for four days and nights, we were faced with a similar situation with a forest fire funneling down the canyon toward our Vision Quest base camp. The similarity is that we both had called in this wind on a very hot and still late spring day to bring relief from the weather. The result was that within ten minutes a strong southern wind arose, blowing continuously for the next four days. Had we been unable to halt that wind in much the same way, then we would have failed the test and it could rightfully be said that we had no business invoking these Element powers. The history of Shamanism on our planet is littered with the casualties of those who tampered with these Primal Forces of Creation and lost control. Great Power must always be accompanied by equally great wisdom.

Fortunately there are built-in safeguards so that the average person seeking to call up such powers is not a threat to themselves or others because they have not yet awakened their powers of "intent."

My first warning was related to the element of Fire and my anger. It was in a board meeting when I became very angry with someone who was challenging my ideas. That evening when he went home, he spilled hot grease on his arm, suffering severe burns. During that same time period, I confronted a man with my anger because he had made false accusations against me. A few hours after my confrontation, he had to be rushed to the hospital with cardiac arrest.

I pondered the meaning of these two episodes for days, wondering if I could possibly have had anything to do with what had happened.

The next two episodes left no doubt in my mind what had happened. I was with my former partner one afternoon as we began the twelve-mile winding drive up the mountain to our home in Highlands, North Carolina. On top of the mountain above us, someone had cleared the vegetation and was constructing a huge three-story vacation house that looked totally out of place in the surrounding mountains and verdant hardwood and pine forests.

So appalled were we that simultaneously we said that we would "like to burn the damn thing down." A few days later we were shocked to discover that indeed it had burned to the ground.

During that same time period we were driving on some back roads in other nearby foothills that led us past a beautiful, peaceful area where some Indian mounds had been left undisturbed in their pristine state.

It was a sacred place, the site of a magnetic vortex, and we had always connected with the energies there.

Once again we were shocked and appalled to discover that two large two-story buildings had been constructed adjacent to the mounds, which were in the midst of a grassy meadow about a hundred feet from a beautiful pristine little river that meandered through the hardwood forest and foothills.

Reacting once more to the inappropriate, opportunistic construction that stood out like a sore thumb against such pastoral surroundings, this time we both exclaimed simultaneously that "somebody should just torch the houses."

Need I describe what happed?   It was a repeat of the former outburst. On our return trip several days later we were shocked to discover that both buildings, which were not even close to each other, had been burned to the ground. We were not the only ones pissed off!

This latter incident was a case of arson, but so upset were we over the fulfillment of our prophetic utterances that we had to enquire if anyone had been hurt. Fortunately not, we were told.

The above episodes occurred at the beginning of the awakening of my "command" over the elements, and I learned an important lesson: the absolute necessity of being in control of the elemental forces within, especially in this case of the fiery essence awakening within me.

One of my mentors, the late Cherokee Medicine Man, Rolling Thunder, once pointed out: "When one's spiritual powers begin awakening, there is a far greater responsibility in that one can cause harm not only to oneself but to those around you!"

These are important teachings I have never forgotten.

Similar teachings existed in Atlantis – the previous great civilization that was destroyed. In the Central Temple of Atlantis, prior to the second great destruction occurring 30,000 years ago, there was kept a sacred book of scientific and psychic law to which only high initiates had access. The book in fact was instrumental in the flowering of that advanced culture. There was a warning in the introduction to the book that is appropriate for every seeker: "Man, when he begins to realize the almost unlimited potential within himself, tends to run too fast, stumbling over his own feet in the process."

Demonstrations

One of the most rewarding experiences Astrid and I have had in working with our students and apprentices has been in our demonstrations. As I described in my book *Soul on Fire*, I had my first vision in 1971 when I was shown the spiritual condition of humanity on this planet as well as my soul purpose in this life. I was told I not only had to remember and awaken my soul powers but also to demonstrate them to others as powers that are latent in all of us. In doing this I would show we are not limited by the laws of the physical plane, but that our very nature is that we are divine and immortal beings without limitations of any kind.

Like nothing else, these demonstrations often were accompanied by a collective euphoria, wonderment and joy as each person present could sense the age-old restrictions and false beliefs lifting off of them, thus allowing them to move into a freer, more expansive view of the world. Seemingly without effort on my part, I was beginning to live my vision.

On a few occasions there was a sense of urgency, such as the time I described earlier when Astrid had to use her intention to stop a thirty-five mile per hour wind that had been blowing continuously for four days and nights.

And yet on another occasion there was the sense of high magic, such as the times I was able to intend several spontaneous combustions of sticks that had been laid for ceremonial fires. On another occasion I was caught with a group of students in a severe electrical storm on a high mountain ridge. We had to pass through a long zone of downed trees struck by lightning during past storms as well as several that had just been torched. Only when we became one with the storm did we find our real protection.

Some of the most remarkable times were when there was opportunity to demonstrate before groups of young people and get them to begin changing their perceptions of the world and who they were. One such demonstration was with a group of graduating senior students of a prep school in the southern United States. In this case, for two nights in a row, I was able to call in thunderstorms which to their amazement each manifested within the hour.

I did a similar demonstration for two days in a row for an eight-year-old boy and his mother by almost instantly materializing thunderstorms. The next thing I was able to demonstrate for him was to persuade a colony of bees that were building nests in the eaves above the doors, to leave almost instantly. This sensitive young man had the opportunity to experience marvels by the standards of the world that would influence him for the rest of his life.

On our vision quests in the Eastern and Western United States, we often called in thunder-storms either to end a drought or for the cleansing and purifying effects these storms had. It was not uncommon for the storm to materialize directly overhead with simultaneous lightning and explosion of thunder. Everyone understood that the phenomenon in itself was not important. What was important was the message that it conveyed: We are beings who are not limited to the laws of the physical plane.

Of course it was a marvel to everyone when we, as a group, were able to achieve such harmony with the natural world through our intentions. One of my favorite times was when we did a ceremony with students in the San Francisco bay area, to block the highly-toxic aerial spraying for the brown apple moth that was supposedly threatening the fruit orchards of northern California. When the spray planes took off for the first time the next morning a dense fog rolled in, quickly grounding the planes. The end result following this failed attempt of a controversial aerial spraying of this area was that the aerial spraying was banned for the entire state of California.

On another occasion while we were camping for four days in the California desert, we twice witnessed dazzling double rainbows formed first around the full moon and then around the noon day sun while we performed ceremonies to protect the badly abused land. True to the promise of these double rainbows the destructive practices in question were banned by the Park Service for the following year.

"Canaries in the Mine Shaft"

As some of you know, Astrid and I have embraced a path of conscious and ecstatic union with all life. That meant we experienced a degree of dissolving of self in becoming one with the flowers of our garden and the great grandmother trees, the dolphin and the whales, the wolf and the feline, the winged ones and the little creatures that hop and crawl about, and finally even the rocks themselves that our Native Americans speak of as the "bones of the Earth Mother" which hold the memories of our Earth and deep wisdom of the stone people.

And whereas this is still a work in progress, we have achieved a sufficient merging to experience ecstatic joy of such a path. Remember that I said that ecstasy is the state that everyone is seeking whether or not they are consciously aware of it.

I never tire of talking about the utter joy Astrid and I both felt when the little dove flew out of the woods and began following her around and finally attempted to nest in her hair. Likewise it filled me with great joy to remember the times deer have come out of the forest and dropped to their knees next to her in total trust. I have experienced a similar ecstatic joy each time I have called up the wind, the thunder, lightning or rain or even the time recently when we called the spirit back into a mockingbird that had died of dehydration.

In attempting to describe the experience of becoming one with these beautiful beings or Elemental powers as well as the spirit of a canyon, a mountain or a desert spring, I am compelled to raise the same question Astrid raised in her introduction to this book: "How does one speak about that for which there are no words?"

The path of ecstatic union with All That Is, is the forgotten path of our humanity. Astrid and I are here to realize this path in our own lives as well as demonstrate to others how it can be achieved.

We believe that we are here to show others where our species is destined to evolve toward – not necessarily in the next generation or even century but much further into the new cycle we are poised to enter in December of 2012.

In developing this unusual degree of unity with all life, we unexpectedly have faced health challenges. We have become extremely sensitive to the electromagnetic frequencies of wi-fi, cell phones and related technology. This opened us to serious health issues.

We have been told by some that we might be the "canaries in the mine shaft." We believe that this is true. It is our opinion that the very thing we are experiencing with the possible toxic effects of this type of radiation, our own Earth and some of the Nature Kingdoms are also experiencing. In this way our sensitivity differs somewhat from the sensitivity of many psychics, mediums and healers. In fact some of these people that I have known seem to feel little connection to the Earth. This is in no way to stand in judgment of them, for they too are a product of our culture. Fortunately most are not that cut off from Nature. There is a growing bit of evidence to support my theory about the toxic effects of electromagnetic frequencies. It seems that we are not alone in the human family in that an increasing number of humans are being affected. For example Sweden now provides for "EMF disability." And that country has already established an EMF-free zone.

One researcher says that, "We are being cooked!" If a frog is placed in boiling water, it jumps out. But if placed in cold water that is gradually heating up, the frog does not realize it is being cooked until it is too late.

Regarding our extreme allergic reactions to electromagnetic radiation, I am sometimes asked the question: "Why can't you and Astrid use your spiritual powers to heal yourselves?" This is not the first time such a question has been asked. Ramakrishna was asked the same question when he was dying of cancer. So was Sri Ramana Maharshi, as have other very advanced souls who died of some form of physical illness. One clue might be found in the ancient tradition of the "wounded healer" who is able to use her powers to heal others but not herself. I did not want to believe this but I am forced to acknowledge that it may have some validity. Perhaps the physical Earth plane has always extracted a certain "tax" from those with special gifts.

It is also known that advanced souls often have many health problems while on Earth because of what they experience as the extremely harsh vibrations of our world in the present cycle. Each of the three times my teacher of a little-known yogic system, the late Paramahansa Janardan, a fully enlightened being, came to America from India he had to return within a few weeks. During each trip to America he became quite ill as a result of the dense and toxic energies of a modern industrial country. I greatly admired the late Paramahansa who is of the same lineage of Yogananda, and I am quite sure that this enlightened soul was not asking himself why he "attracted" or "created" this, or why he needed to "own" this as many on spiritual paths are so fond of saying today. This is not to say that such concepts do not have some validity, but we have a tendency to absolutize relative truth and in so doing miss a great opportunity for growth.

The Ring of Power

It may be that we, like the Atlanteans before us, may be taking a wrong turn with our total embrace of technology. We have become attached to our computers and cell phones without regard for the mounting evidence that the radiation from these toys may pose a threat to more and more life forms on Earth as well as the health of many humans. We have to ask ourselves why we have the sudden dying off of a growing number of species of birds, bats and bees.

Many people become angry and defensive when it is suggested that we may have to invest large sums of capital to develop shields and other means of protecting ourselves and the environment against the possible toxic effects of wi-fi and cell phone towers. Worse still are governments of the world and covert military groups that are experimenting with devices to control the weather and cause earthquakes. The point is that this obsession with technology to do everything for us represents a wrong turn in our human evolution on this planet. All of this is about power that is outside of us when we should be focusing on the power that is within.

Consider this: If at least a few of us have already developed the power to heal, to call up or stop the winds, to call in storms, to end droughts even from across the country, to instantly stop torrential rain, to combust ceremonial fires, to repeatedly clear the pollution out of an area with a radius of twenty to thirty miles, to move objects from one place to another or to transport our bodies from one place to another, *then what else is possible?*

It is apparent to me that there is a power within each of us that is without limits. In spite of the fact that only a few have learned to tap this ability, it is available to all. What if this power within could be used as a source of energy to warm or light up buildings, to run computers, or even travel through space? This energy would be nonpolluting, renewable, cost-free and available to all people, even those with little means. Most importantly it is a power that cannot be taken away from us because it is a part of who and what we are.

There is no personal growth gained by relying on the present technology of our culture. This technology in and of itself does not bring about personal growth. Whereas by learning to tap the power within each of us, there is enormous growth and unlimited possibilities for the advancement of our consciousness.

By embracing technology and ignoring the almost untapped energy source within ourselves we are failing to choose the high road. We have chosen a path where there is little advancement in the evolution of our consciousness and increasing possibilities of harm to our health and ultimately to the destruction of all life on this planet.

Atlantis went under because of misuse of a technology far more advanced than our own. It was destroyed because many became obsessed with developing power outside of themselves which in the end they were unable to control. The Atlantean people lost control of their lives, allowing more and more of the power, wealth and knowledge to fall into the hands of a small, elitist group. Ultimately it was secrecy that destroyed Atlantis, as is happening today. It is our greatest present evil.

Awakening our soul powers and commanding the elements, cannot happen apart from our being able to control and balance the primal forces within each one of us. Too many today are not living in the moment but for the moment.

Years ago I was told that my life purpose was to remember, awaken, teach and then demonstrate the existence of this power that is within each of us. I have subsequently demonstrated this on numerous occasions, as have Astrid and now some of our apprentices. It is up to others like us to find new applications of this power, the source of which is the divine spark within all of us.

I am speaking of a power and knowledge that no government or elitist group can take away from us because it is within.

There is an old story that I once heard about a king who realized there was going to be a revolution, and that his kingdom would be overthrown and he would die. So he took his newborn son to a trusted farmer and said, "Take my son and raise him as your own, but when he becomes a man, give him my ring which is a symbol of sovereign power in our land. Say to him, "You are not my son but the son of the king! Take this ring and go claim that which is yours by divine right."

Imagine how this young man must have felt. But we can readily see that this is a story about each one of us when we set out to claim what is rightfully ours. Just as I chose to claim that well-known promise of the Nazarene: "Greater things than these shall you be able to do." So I now say to you, go and claim what is your birthright and entitlement.

The Path toward Oneness

There is a story about the East Indian master of the last century, Ramakrishna. It is about a time he was with his disciples on the Ganges River. They had just observed two men on a raft floating down the river in front of them get involved in a knife fight. As they were slashing at each other, the disciples became horrified, not knowing what to do. There was no way to intervene. To their astonishment when they looked over at their master, he too was bleeding. Everywhere a knife had struck one of the men, Ramakrishna was bleeding. This master was so connected to everyone around him that he felt and experienced the pain and the wounding of others.

When I first read this story, I was amazed that anyone could have such extreme sensitivity. Today as a result of several personal experiences, I am no longer amazed. A little less than two decades ago I was staying at a motel in Joshua Tree National Monument in California. Around ten o'clock that night, as I was getting ready to fall asleep, I felt and heard something pop in the lower part of my abdominal area. Almost immediately I felt fluid rushing up from that part of my body into the chest and lung area. As this happened, I said to myself, "I know that this is death that I am feeling." I was certain that it was my own death, but it made no sense because I had had no health problems remotely related to that kind of experience. When I decided to call 911, I discovered that I was unable to move my arms over to the telephone. It was as if they were paralyzed. Finally I said to myself, "If I am to die this way and at this time, then so be it". I let go completely. I released my fears and all resistance. To my astonishment the moment I did this the feeling of paralysis began to rapidly diminish, and I began to be aware that I was experiencing someone else's health condition. Within a minute or two I realized that this was a good friend who was living in North Carolina. She had assisted me with my rehabilitation following a heart attack and had offered me a place to stay on her father's horse ranch.

Knowing that she was in trouble, I called her even though it would have been two o'clock in the morning her time. As soon as she picked up the phone, I told my friend she needed to get to a hospital right away. She explained to me that she had been having pains in her abdominal area and had spent the day at the hospital emergency room with her sister, but after eight hours, when they had not got to her, they both got tired of waiting and came home. I told my friend that she needed to go back right away because she was in danger.

In spite of my exhortations she waited until the next day to go to the hospital where it was discovered that her appendix had ruptured the night before. And peritonitis had gone all the way up into her lungs, preventing her from getting enough oxygen to the brain even while on a respirator. The result was that there was brain damage and sadly the family had to pull the tubes and let her die. She was one who had always enjoyed life and lived it to its fullest. To go on living with severe brain damage would have been unacceptable to her.

Even with the power of this knowledge it is not always possible to help the ones we love. Fortunately I have been more successful with others. Another story I wish to share occurred a few years ago when Astrid and I were living in a home in the little town of Townsend outside of Knoxville. One afternoon I suddenly got a strong sense that I needed to get up and do a ceremony to protect Astrid. I did not know where she was or what she was doing at the time, but I knew that she was in great danger. It turned out that fifteen minutes after I did the ceremony for Astrid, she was in a three car collision. Miraculously she was unhurt, when she easily could have been killed. I am convinced that the warning I received and the ceremony I did gave her the protection that she needed, and perhaps the protection the people in the other car needed as well.

One morning a few months after Astrid's near fatal episode I awoke feeling great concern for a woman living in the our area who was a gifted medium and spiritual teacher. It was about three o'clock in the morning and it was without a doubt that she had been in some kind of danger. I got up and did a ceremony for her. It later turned out she had been in great danger at the time and was convinced that what I did helped to save her life.

I learned that the opportunity to help fellow human beings becomes much greater when we realize that we are inseparably a part of them and a part of their lives. We could miss such opportunities if we are still locked in the consciousness of separation that has infected most of the people in our world. I have had many more experiences similar to these, but perhaps I have made my point. This should give you some idea of what can happen when we begin surrendering our individuality, realizing the oneness we seek is no metaphor. Today we are in a unique period in history in which we as a human race are shifting from a state of separation and fragmentation into unity and oneness. We discover that there is but one life, one pulse, one heart beat that exists throughout all Creation. Each one of us is a part of that oneness.

I have said the forgotten path of our human species is that of ecstatic union with all life and we are showing our students and apprentices how to merge with the mountain and river spirit, the tree devas and the powers of Fire, Air and Water and to experience the euphoria of becoming one with the plants in their garden, the creatures of the wild and their fellow humans.

Chapter 8: Forging the Immortal KA (Ascension Body)

Ecstasy, Primal Power, and the Development of the KA

The great alchemical work for our humanity in the new millennium is that of forging the Immortal KA or Ascension Body, or what the native peoples of the Americas think of as the *Nahua*.

Earlier in this text I shared stories of experiences of this extraordinary phenomenon. These included appearing in this form one Sunday morning in my dentist's home to warn him of an electrical fire in his basement. Another episode was that of being transported one night to the home of an apprentice at the time he was verbally crying out to me for help. He nearly fainted when seconds later I actually appeared in his apartment and began speaking with him. On another occasion, when I was with a group of eighteen apprentices on a wilderness outing, I suddenly teleported to a nearby trailhead when one of our members urgently needed my help.

In every instance I was seen and heard by others and could be touched as well. Had I been walking in sand or snow, no doubt there would have been footprints. Unlike the astral body, which makes no impact on the physical world, clearly this surprising ability of mine was not astral or thought projection, but it was an appearance of my double, which is sometimes called the KA or the Radiant Body, the Ascension Body or the *Nahual* of Toltec tradition. This vehicle is capable of transporting me, or anyone else for that matter, instantly over great distances and even appearing in other forms such as the huge white eagle, which appeared out of nowhere while my author friend and her acquaintance were discussing me. They watched with amazement as it flew toward them, alighting in a nearby eight hundred year old live oak.

For thousands of years the development of the KA was an essential part of advanced spiritual practices, for it is the permanent vehicle that enables one to move through different planes, dimensions and spaces, as well as to bilocate or teleport in the physical world, as many Atlanteans were so adept at doing.

The KA will be the vehicle we will use as we move more fully into a fifth dimensional Earth. In the coming generation, therefore, we can expect great emphasis on developing our KA as part of our advanced spiritual practices.

At the time of the first century the world had become a violent and terrible place in which to live. Much of the ancient knowledge and practices of developing the KA, such as existed in ancient Egypt, were in danger of being forever lost. The Romans had destroyed many of the ancient cultures and along with that the ancient records and libraries. The Masters saw that a great spiritual crisis on a planetary scale was in the making. If this knowledge were to be lost, it could greatly set back human evolution on this planet. Their response to this impending threat was to send two great Masters, Buddha and Yeshua. Yeshua came to demonstrate beyond doubt the existence of the KA and that we all survive physical death. On the other hand, Buddha faithfully rediscovered and taught the means of developing the KA. So Buddhism and Christianity are part of the same body of knowledge.

I have said that the KA is formed by the imprinting of our essence with experience. The more intense the experience, the greater the imprinting of our double, which is the raw material for the KA. It is this imprinting that gives form to the amorphous egg-shaped double. That form, of course, is our physical appearance.

Giving form to one's double therefore requires discipline, strict attention, and "presence." I have taught and demonstrated a powerful aid to the development of the KA. It is that of the ecstatic and conscious union with the creation itself. This is perhaps the most natural way as opposed to the more formal practices of Buddhism and Western Mystery School traditions.

We are creatures who evolved out of close interaction with the Natural World. For this reason Astrid and I claim that an ecstatic union with all life, if combined with the above disciplines, is our modern "short path" to self-realization. In a sense this truth is so self-evident it has escaped most of us in these modern times. I am continually amazed at how many students I have encountered who are working with advanced practices but feel little or no connection with the natural world. This is not their fault, but simply a reflection of our modern, secular culture.

Unlike the physical body, the KA is made of quantum light particles that are both conscious and ecstatic. We are here in this unprecedented time to forge our KA or Ascension Body. For those who, like me, came in with a fully developed KA, there is great opportunity to increase that ecstasy, as there is no limit to the amount of ecstasy that our Ascension Body can carry.

As ecstasy is added, our light increases. A Master for example will have a field of brilliant light. If a soul is very advanced, then the KA can be both visible and solid. One can do almost anything that can be accomplished in the physical body and much, much more.

For Astrid and me that awakened ecstatic joy has become increasingly a part of our daily experience of Nature and the Earth. To observe a family of deer or an elk herd in the wild, to listen to the dove ushering in the morning, to watch, hear, smell and feel the ecstasy of an approaching summer storm, to listen to the sound of a rushing stream, or the wind in the trees – all these awaken that very high vibratory quality of ecstasy.

It is important to remember that ecstatic joy, like love, is not something we have to get from outside of ourselves. It is who and what we are. It is only that we have forgotten this; as the memories return to us, then we know with certitude.

This may surprise some of you, but the vibration of ecstatic joy is higher than the frequency of divine compassion or universal love. This can be explained as follows: the vibration of ecstatic joy is so all-inclusive that it contains the frequencies of love, forgiveness, oneness, bliss and inner harmony. It is the highest vibration in the manifest universe, because of the fact that ecstasy is the combined essence of all the other frequencies that make up what has been spoken of as the gifts of the Spirit.

So try it! Go out into the world of Nature. Observe the diversity and the beauty of whatever is experienced. Feel that magic, the calm, the nurturing, the sounds of silence, the sounds of the elements themselves. Now let go of the old program of separation and become one with what you are experiencing.

One more thought, and here again is where both Eastern and Western traditions have missed a most important point. The portal into higher states of consciousness is that of the primal. Nature, of course, is primal. A shaman's command over the elements is her command over the Primal Forces of Creation. Remember this: power comes from below; higher wisdom comes from above. Indigenous shamans connect with their power not through beautiful guided meditations, but through drums, didgeridoos, primal dancing, chanting, rattles, overtones and devices like the Tibetan bowls that set up resonances within your being.

In our travels around the country, Astrid and I have been shocked to discover how many people have been studying for twenty or thirty years using spiritual practices they learned from teachers and yet were not much closer to enlightenment than when they started. We believe that what was missing was knowing how to move through that portal to access the primal power of Creation itself. It is through the portal of the primal that we can access the transcendental. Perhaps this is one of the reasons that few of our Western teachers, who in some cases have written and spoken elegantly about truth of the highest order, have not experienced any extensive awakening of their soul powers.

The KA or Ascension Body can only be developed through our shift from the mind to the heart space. This shift is the cosmic mandate for the New Cycle we are entering, because if we remain trapped in our mind and artificial self, we are doomed.

With the development of the conscious mind, we experienced separation for the first time. Separation in itself was essential to the development of our individuality. However, in experiencing this separation for the formation of the "I" or "ego," we were always to remember the essential oneness and unity from which we had sprung and to which we were someday to return. That oneness and unity, of course, were and always will be our primary reality.

Of course, the above remembrance did not happen. We forgot who we were, and began playing the game of separation. The idea of oneness became a distant echo we could scarcely remember. This separation is the source of all our suffering in this world.

In our identification with the rational mind and separation from the heart space and intuitive mind, an artificial self was developed. It is important to understand that the rational mind is not an aspect of the soul, which is the "cumulative consciousness of our evolving spirit or essence." The mind is a "tool of consciousness" – one of a number of tools, but not consciousness itself. A person may be gifted with a brilliant mind but might not be highly evolved if they have difficulty understanding higher truth.

Our culture has identified with this tool, believing it to be the real self. The result of this misperception was that an artificial self was formed. For this reason many indigenous tribes of the Americas, Australia and Africa found Europeans almost incomprehensible, and began speaking of us as "mutants" or referring to themselves as the "real people," such as the highly advanced Kogi people of South America. The following are some of the unique characteristics of the artificial self that has been created by our identification with the rational mind:

1. When ruled by the artificial self, we became time-bound for the first time. We began living primarily in the past or future, seldom in the present moment. This was exactly the opposite of what was intended and what we once knew.
2. We knew separation for the first time and suddenly we had enemies. It was "us against them." And so there arose the need for defense.
3. We began living apart from Nature, eventually perceiving it as a threat or at least something to lord over and use as we saw fit.
4. For the first time God existed outside of ourselves and soon became "a god created in our own image," and worse, as we

see so prevalent today, God became "the One God divided against Itself."

5. We felt it necessary to defend not just our home and children, but our ideas, beliefs, character and reputation.

6. In our separation from the heart, we no longer knew what was right as we once had. For the first time we needed rules to live by and began enacting more and more laws to enforce those rules.

7. We began living in a "survival mentality" and a "fear-based society." The artificial emotion of fear is possible only when we are living in the future. I speak not of a natural, concrete, tangible fear such as we would experience if a tiger were in the room, but an unnatural, abstract fear of what might or could happen.

I have already spoken about the fact that we are here to increase ecstasy. The Ascension Body, unlike our physical vehicle, is made of subatomic particles that are both conscious and ecstatic. What then is this ecstasy that all are seeking either consciously or unconsciously? There are a number of cases of spontaneous ecstasy experienced under great duress, such as the soldier on the battlefield, who in the midst of his terror is suddenly overcome by a sense of profound peace or ecstatic joy. What is actually happening is that this person is remembering who he is as an immortal, spiritual being. Others have experienced this phenomena in near-death experiences, or perhaps when visiting some religious shrine. The problem is that almost invariably they decide to write a book about it, go on the lecture circuit, or appear on as many talk shows as they can. They become self-appointed authorities of this divine, supernal experience.

What most of these persons have failed to do is to discover how they can achieve that sublime state of consciousness at will. Obviously the soldier is not meant to re-enlist or get on another battlefield to have that same experience. The runner is at a disadvantage if she can only experience that runner's high while running to the point of exhaustion. The mountain climber and those engaged in extreme sports also may experience a kind of high, but they too are greatly limited in the ways that high can be accessed. Likewise, the religious person is limited if they can only experience a group high in some kind of uplifting religious service.

Why not seek out spiritual practices that can enable us to access these sublime states over and over again? That is the directive from on High for our New Cycle.

These practices require discipline, commitment and presence, but so few seem willing to make such a choice. And, of course, there is the added ingredient I have given that can greatly accelerate such practices, which is through our conscious unity with the creation.

Are there examples of people whose enlightenment was inseparably connected to that ecstatic union with all life? Saint Francis comes to mind, also ecstatic and visionary thirteenth-century German nun Hildegard von Bingen. Both of these great lights experienced ecstatic union with the creation, and there are many more whose names are not as well known.

I began this chapter by saying that the great alchemical work for our humanity in the beginning of the New Cycle is that of forging the Immortal Ascension Body, or KA.

Alchemy for practitioners in the Middle Ages was about discovering the means for changing base metal into gold. Its deeper meaning is that gold is the element of the soul while the egg-shaped etheric double, which is seated in the lowest chakra, represents the base metal or raw material which through spiritual practice can be transmuted into the Immortal Ascension Body.

One living Master recently has said that "our humanity's return to the Earth will be its Ascension." Astrid and I concur. This is why we emphasize with such passion and zeal that your growing unity from lengthy observation, involvement, and gratitude for all life on this planet will take you on a spiritual ride faster than the Hadron Particle Accelerator of Berne, Switzerland could ever do with those tiny photons.

My "White Eagle" Connection

On dozens of occasions over the last three decades, I have appeared to people in the dream or visionary state as a huge white eagle. Usually those appearances are accompanied by the messages: "I am Peter Calhoun. I am your teacher." Or simply "I am White Eagle." Or "I am Snow Eagle," which is the way I am known among indigenous tribes. Some have guessed correctly that I was the Apostle John who has always been identified with that symbol.

The eagle, however, is connected with my High Self as well as that of the Apostle. My personal belief is that "White Eagle" is actually a "collective" of souls from the Sirius star system. The Apostle John is, of course, the best known member of that collective among people in our culture. As you, my readers, will recall, I was given the task of remembering all of my past lives. The memories of the Christ Drama of the first century are lucid to me and later I wish to say something more about that time period that has been so misunderstood.

Materializing the Double

I have been asked how I appeared to my author friend and her friend as a huge white eagle that was definitely of a type of physical substance, and, therefore, not a thought projection or a dream image. My answer would be that all of us are multidimensional beings; any of us could materialize in another form once we let go of the need to be a certain person or even the need to always be in our human form. In so doing we must be at the point in our development where we have come into an understanding that *we are all things*.

The second understanding for materializing in a different location in our human form is the recognition that space as distance is an illusion, and there is no real separation.

It is this same concept that will be the key to telepathic communication which will become the norm in the fifth dimensional world that is in the offering. For most people this will not happen immediately after the "Shift of the Ages" occurs with the alignment of December 21, 2012. Rather it will manifest first with a few and then more and more will develop it. The real key, of course, will be when our children are taught this and are never exposed to the false belief that there is separation of any kind.

Chapter 9: The Ripple Effect in Action

PART 1: A Key Concept for Our Time

Illuminating Truth

In every age there are a number of ideas and truths that capture the popular imagination and have the effect of uplifting our mass consciousness. But there are a few key ideas which, if introduced at a critical time, have the power to transform the world, elevating us into a new level of awareness. In order to distinguish these from the more common ideas we are familiar with, let us refer to these as illuminating truths or "illuminators." So potent are these illuminators that we can liken them to the burst of a super nova on the landscape of the collective consciousness of our race.

It has long been known that these illuminators must be introduced within a very narrow window of time. If that tiny portal of opportunity is missed, the chance for a major leap in consciousness is lost and a vast amount of time can elapse before such an opportunity appears again. Precision timing then is of paramount importance for an illuminator to take hold in the mass consciousness.

All this has to do with the understanding of how cycles work. We know that time is an illusion, but cycles are very real. There are cycles within cycles within cycles within cycles. This is how everything in our Infinite Creation evolves and changes. It has been said "everything is in the process of becoming something it is not." At the completion of each cycle, if the appropriate lessons are learned, we make a leap into a higher cycle, thus making up the spiral of evolution.

If we wish to insert an illuminator into Earth's time stream, we need to know the exact point at which that narrow portal will open and for how long. I believe that the time is now right for the insertion of such an illuminator. We might liken this to a surfer who waits to catch the crest of the largest wave that will propel him effortlessly to shore. It is what Shakespeare meant when he wrote about a "tide in the affairs of men which taken at its crest leads on to fame and fortune." Shakespeare continues by pointing out the tragic state of affairs should the crest of that tide be missed. Sadly, that will be the fate of our species, should we miss the unprecedented opportunity that looms before us. We will still reach our destination, but there will be much struggle, suffering, and a vastly longer journey.

It does not require that large numbers of people be aware of such an illuminating truth. Ordinarily only a small percentage of the total population is needed to achieve critical mass yet when that critical mass is reached, there is an explosion of consciousness such that everyone's reality is changed.

For most the shift in perception occurs on the unconscious level, but the effects of this shift, if we could perceive it in our inner vision, are dazzling to behold. Like a floodlight placed on a darkened landscape, our whole perception of who we are is transformed and a truth we never knew about is suddenly illuminated.

The following statements describe the nature of such illuminators:
1. There is ordinarily a very narrow window of opportunity in which an illuminator can take root in the mass consciousness; it is essential to know exactly when and where this illuminator can be inserted into the time stream.
2. A relatively small percentage of the total population realizing the illuminating truth is usually enough to achieve critical mass. it is similar to the hundredth-monkey effect.
3. An illuminator seldom becomes a popular idea, yet it deeply inspires and transforms a few who recognize it for what it is.
4. An illuminator tends to bypass the intellect, taking root in the deeper levels of the mind.
5. An illuminator is not an abstract belief but a living truth.
6. An illuminator is not a static concept but a dynamic principal.
7. An illuminator needs not so much to be understood by the mind but to be lived.
8. For an illuminator, articulating it and demonstrating it is one and the same. The demonstrating is the teaching.

9. An illuminator is like a seed which, when planted in the soil, remains unseen for a time and later bursts into the light of day.
10. Some examples of these illuminators are:
    a. Loving one's neighbor as oneself
    b. Returning good for evil
    c. Being present in the now
    d. Equal protection under the law
    e. The relationship of energy, matter and the speed of light
    f. That life, liberty and the pursuit of happiness are inalienable rights for all people.

All of the above were considered radical or untrue at the time they were introduced, and yet they ultimately changed the way we perceived ourselves and our world.

As I have said in the preceding pages, the "illuminator" I wish to introduce is found in the title of this book: *Life Without Limits*. In other words we are beings who by our very nature are reflections of the One Creator. Because we are manifestations of the Creator, we are without limitations of any kind. The difficulty however is that we continually self-impose all kinds of limitations based on our false perceptions of ourselves and the world. I have described how each of us has accepted a false belief system that has resulted in our leading lives that are limiting and inconsequential. This belief system has made up the consensus reality of every major culture in every age for the last five thousand years or more.

The result of the above scenario is that most people in our world are living in a veritable prison, a prison of the mind. The good news is that our Earth prison is a prison without walls, and we are free to walk out of it at any time. This truth was graphically reflected in the recurring dream I had most of my life about being in a prison in which one whole wall was missing, and people could walk out at anytime, but no one ever did.

I have repeatedly pointed out that this confinement is the result not of our ignorance but of the greatest deception in the history of our species. So effective was this deception that was put in place by the "controllers" of our world that even they were amazed. It was indeed a masterful plan, but one that has run its course, as a rapidly growing number of our species wish to know the truth that sets all beings free.

Therefore some of us, as we speak, are beginning to dismantle this prison by calling attention to this great deception and challenging the false beliefs of our time. You are invited to join us in this unprecedented bid for freedom, for it is freedom that is the very nature of the soul. Let us now examine more closely some of the amazing changes occurring in our time and the opportunity for us to seize the day.

Breaking Free of Spiritual Gravity

One day in the near future an extraordinarily brilliant mind will unlock the secrets of magnetism, and we will be launched into the true Space Age. From this moment on our species will be forever changed. We will have come to know that we are part of a much greater reality than that of our own little blue and white pearl in the sky we call Earth. Through the discovery of those magnetic vectors which scientists speak of as worm holes, we will be able to visit not only the nearest stars but those that are vast numbers of light years away. As incomprehensible as it may seem, these mysterious magnetic anomalies will be able to transport us almost instantly to stars whose light will not reach our Earth for a million years. This will be the scientific discovery of the millennium, because no longer will our species be Earthbound. We will be forever free of the gravitational forces of our planet.

The Universe Within

Perhaps some of you, like me, find such concepts as the above incredibly exciting and mind expanding. In Spiritual Science, however, it has long been known that knowledge of the greater universe without, as fascinating as it can be, does not compare in importance to knowledge of the universe within ourselves.

Many years ago when I was asking a teacher question after question about the vastness of the Creation, I was asked: "Why do you seek to know that which is beyond, and beyond and beyond when you do not even know that Universe that is in yourself?" I got the message! Since that time, my effort has been to know the Universe that is within.

Springing the Trap

In the preceding pages I have described an even greater discovery we are on the verge of making, which I have said pertains to the elusive Universe within. In much the same way the Illuminating Truth that is the theme of this book has the power to spring us out of this Earth prison, this prison of the mind, and free us from the false belief systems that we as a species have accepted. Elsewhere I have said that these limiting belief systems are the chains that bind us and the prison walls that contain us. When our species comes to realize that we are beings who are without limitations of any kind, our whole reality will have changed dramatically. The way we perceive ourselves and our world will be so different. We will wonder how we could have failed to discern this truth about ourselves.

I say once more without reservation: the concept that we are beings who are without limitations is one of the great illuminating truths of the ages. The discovery and acceptance of this illuminator has dramatically changed my life and Astrid's. Now it is changing the lives of a growing number of our students and those they are reaching. This is the ripple effect in action.

As a result of the stories in *Soul on Fire*, along with my lectures and public demonstrations and the inspired writings of some of my colleagues, there is the beginning of a "groundswell" of people breaking free from the prison of false beliefs. These individuals are demonstrating in their own way that we are not limited to the laws of the physical plane. As others realize what is possible, they go and do likewise, creating a ripple effect.

The New Shamanism

At first I thought I was one of those teachers bringing back the precepts of traditional shamanism, the oldest system of knowledge on the planet. With the future of many species on Earth in peril, including our human species, I felt that shamanism was an important key to the healing of our Earth and mankind.

Since that time the new shamanism has become a worldwide movement, and hardly a week goes by without my meeting a person who claims to be a shaman or speaks about their personal shaman.

In time I became increasingly aware that Astrid and I were bringing in a type of magic that was revolutionary. Examples of this magic, which to my knowledge is not found in traditional shamanism, include the ability I describe in several of the stories in *Soul on Fire*, of being able to walk into a herd or family of wild animals; Astrid's' experiences of having deer walk up to her and drop to their knees as if to visit with her while gazing at her in total trust; or the wild dove that flew out of the trees and attempted to nest in her hair. There are no words for me to describe the effect these episodes with Astrid had on me. I knew that such things were extraordinary even by my standards. Truly there are no limits to what is possible. Then there are numerous instances when we have been able to call many different species to us, including deer, bears, cougars, bobcats, eagles, bison, black snakes and even a tiny moth or praying mantis. Also there were my experiences of self-combusting and of being the recipient of a full lightning strike without being harmed. And unprecedented are the times we have been able to clear the pollution out of an area of a thirty-mile radius extending over a two week period. One episode I have yet to mention but which may be worth noting as a means of dealing with the current increase of blight and insect infestation in Nature was the successful attempt I made of healing the diseased and dying hemlock trees on my property. It was simply through my verbalizing my intentions several times that the blight disappeared and was replaced by new growth and at this point has not returned. What we were bringing in can be summed up by the phase that we are beings without limitations.

In my first book *Soul on Fire* I told a number of true stories that, taken individually, prove little; but together imply that we are beings who are not limited by the laws of the physical plane as we have been taught to believe. Now in *Life Without Limits* I have stated specifically what I implied in my first book: that we are beings who are limited only by our perception of who we are and of the Earth.

PART 2: Current Accomplishments of a Few Apprentices

I was delighted when Astrid began demonstrating her own soul powers that included a command over the elements of Earth, Air and Water. In a previous chapter I have described her awakening and accomplishments. Since that time we have witnessed a growing number of students and apprentices also awakening to their soul powers. I will now describe for you some of their accomplishments:

One afternoon we were gathered with our apprentices in a cabin in the Smokey Mountains, when we found ourselves studying several recent photos of Taylor, who had been with us for about a year. Taylor is an organic farmer who raises several thousand cattle and chickens as well as a handful of bison and elk for the market. He is part of a new breed of farmers attempting to work within the laws of Nature to bring in the element of compassion for all life. So connected is he with his animals that he prays over each one and smudges them before they are killed. At no time do they experience fear or suffering.

Taylor is part of a talented and diversified group of adults who have been studying with Astrid and me for the past year or more. We have chosen them to be worthy exemplars of the illuminating truth that each one of us is a being without limitations. They are living out the truth implicit in Jesus's great promise that I decided to test several decades ago: "Greater things than these shall ye be able to do."

These apprentices are demonstrating a promise I made to them, that powers similar to those that awakened in Astrid and me would awaken in them. Some of our students surprised themselves when what we promised began to actually happen.

Despite my strong belief in this illuminating truth, I was filled with utter joy and the deepest gratitude by what I was witnessing. After several decades I could finally say to myself: "I have truly lived out the impossible dream that was my vision. Thank you, thank you a thousand times over."

There were extraordinary photos of Taylor standing in the middle of a large council fire. Under ordinary circumstances a fire that size would have consumed his cloth coveralls in a matter of seconds and caused severe burns. But these were not ordinary circumstances. Taylor stood totally unharmed amidst of the flames for more than five minutes. For Taylor, who had always had an excessive fear of fire, it was as if a power suddenly welled up from within, enabling of him to step into the flames. According to Taylor he felt as if he were hovering slightly above his head, observing the phenomenon with detachment.

When I first described my own personal path to "command of the elements," which is an ancient and impeccable path to self-realization that is found in both Vedic and shamanic traditions throughout the world, and stated that we would teach our apprentices how to awaken their own abilities, Taylor had commented to me that he had always had a fear of fire. I told him about the shamanic belief that what we resist, avoid or fear is the place of our greatest power.

Only a few months prior to this fire episode, Taylor had begun having extraordinary visitations by owls. He soon realized that the owl was his totem animal and that he could use his owl medicine to attempt the healing of a friend who had been totally blinded in an accident and informed by his doctors that he might never see again. No one could have been more surprised than Taylor himself when this fortunate individual found his eyesight fully restored the very next day.

The same healing ability that emerged in Taylor appeared to work with horses, as well. Taylor's favorite horse, a three-year-old-gelding named Buckeye, had contracted olieisis, a disease with symptoms similar to colic, but more serious and usually fatal. When Taylor decided to spiritually intervene as a last minute attempt to save Buckeye, the horse had already been lying on his side for several hours. During this time the gelding had grown increasingly weaker with more and more labored breathing. According to Taylor, at this stage death is almost certain and the horse usually has only a few hours to live.

Not to be deterred by the vet who wanted to put Buckeye down, Taylor went over and stooped down beside Buckeye's head. He intoned a Sanskrit mantra I had recently given him to accelerate his spiritual powers. It was through direct revelation that Taylor knew the mantra was what was needed for Buckeye's healing.

Upon completing the intonation, Taylor slapped the gelding on the neck with his hand. To the amazement of several people who were witnessing this, Buckeye leapt to his feet and began prancing around the corral as if nothing had happened.

"It was truly amazing," Taylor said. "To me it seems more miraculous than the healing of the person who had lost his eyesight."

I have taken the liberty of describing the diversity of abilities that have begun to unfold in just one of our apprentices, but Taylor was not alone in this amazing transformation. Never have our apprentices been competitive with one another; they love to hear Shaman stories of other students, not just of Astrid and me. They are inspired by one another's successes and recognize that each have their own talents to bring forth.

There is however a justifiable pride one has in new-found powers. One apprentice, after returning from a training session, went hiking with a close friend the following week in the Rockies. When the friend asked a little skeptically what she had learned with those crazy shamans, she demonstrated by successfully calling up the Winds. Within seconds following her summons, while she faced the East the winds sprang up and began gusting with increasing velocity. Then at his request, wondering if she had just been lucky in her timing, she was able to bring the wind to an immediate and complete standstill. I think she actually surprised herself by her success in her first attempt at commanding the Air element.

I point out some of the accomplishments of other students and apprentices because individually these examples and stories prove little, but taken as a whole they provide a blazing testimonial to long hidden truth about ourselves.

Recently another talented apprentice, Jonathan, called me about his work with the weather spirits. It was a natural focus for this apprentice, an anthropologist, in as much as he had a large organic garden.

"I have made three attempts to call in the rain this season and each one was successful beyond my wildest expectation," he said. "In fact that is an appropriate word because each storm was accompanied by wild spectacular displays of thunder and lightning. At times it appeared as if the lightning intended to hit me as it kept striking so close. The last storm began with the lightning striking no more than fifty feet away from me with a simultaneous explosion of thunder and lightning."

Astrid and I could not help but erupt in convulsive laughter because, as we explained to Jonathan, it was a perfect description of some of our own experiences of calling in the storm devas. I reassured Jonathan that the storm spirits meant no harm. This was simply their signature, letting him know that they were aware of him and wished to serve him. "All indications are that you are a Lightening Shaman like me," I said. Our Native American friends believed that to be the most powerful kind of shaman.

Another apprentice, Danielle, had immediate success communicating and negotiating with her animal friends. Her first attempt was with two different species of bees that invaded her premises. In her first attempt to negotiate with these wonderful little beings, she managed to convince them to quickly move to another location. She also managed to get the coyotes in her neighborhood to stop preying on her neighbor's cats and dogs, convincing them that there was more than enough food out in the wild.

In addition, Danielle has had some amazing successes in combining her natural healing gift with the healing modality she learned from Astrid and me. One of her greatest triumphs has been with her husband Todd, a trainer/presenter who speaks before large audiences. Eight years earlier he had been stricken with severe anxiety attacks. In his own words, "If on a scale of one to ten, passing out was a ten, then mine were all nines."

Todd's anxiety attacks were extreme and frequent. Mainstream methods like psychotherapy, hypnosis and anti-anxiety medications virtually had no effect. Danielle, using the trauma removal method we described, was able to precipitate, within minutes, a complete healing. Todd continues to enjoy a life free of the intense anxiety he had experienced over an eight-year period.

Another instantaneous healing occurred with a woman who had always been terrified of driving across bridges. On one occasion she was forced to have a policeman drive her automobile across a series of bridges because she was paralyzed with fear. To her amazement all fear vanished after Danielle's healing, and she is unable to this day to experience the former emotion that would leave her paralyzed with anxiety. It should be pointed out that once the energetic imprint has been dissolved, the original extreme emotion cannot be reproduced.

It would be misleading to suggest that the only people who have awakened their spiritual talent are apprenticing with Astrid and me. One woman, inspired by one of my stories in *Soul on Fire*, e-mailed me about the energetic dome of light she placed over her organic garden three years in a row, with dramatic results. Not a single bite was taken out of it. Each year her less fortunate neighbors, whose gardens had been ravaged, begged her to tell them what kind of spray she was using. Of course they did not believe her when she told them about her unconventional method.

That season the same woman was experiencing a drought in her area. She off-handedly said as she walked back into her home, "Let there be a storm." The skies were clear at the time and no rain was in sight. Thirty minutes later she saw a blinding flash of light and heard a deafening clap of thunder directly overhead. By the next day, the drought was over.

Another apprentice: Cary, an architect who had been designing the top floor of the Trump Tower in Chicago using sacred geometry, also began awakening extraordinary healing talents while involved with our program. He began to be able to identify past lives of those people in need of his services when these were the source of their present day problems. At the time of the writing of this chapter, Cary is in the process of completing a book describing some of the dramatic healings that are past-life related entitled, *The Power of Karma and Healing*. Cary's first healing was with a woman he had just met, who was dying of a rare blood disease that had resisted all medical treatments. This was followed by the instantaneous healing of a woman who had been suffering from severe non-stop headaches for the past two years, an affliction that had failed to respond to treatment by medical professionals, energy medicine healers and a world-famous healer from South America. Using the revolutionary healing technology Cary learned through our program, it took approximately twenty minutes for him to initiate a complete healing for the tearful and amazed woman, who experienced an immediate and total transformation. Later her puzzled doctors confirmed what she already knew, that she was completely healed. Cary, who has researched and studied numerous healing modalities, has stated that the healing modality Astrid and I teach is by the far the most rapid and the most effective method of healing he has even known. "It is truly an amazing protocol," he said.

Cary has produced several moving DVDs describing some of the amazing healings he facilitated, including a woman who had lost both kidneys and was rejecting a donor kidney. In the DVD the client herself describes the healing that was also accompanied by the disappearance of hip and back pain.

Using other techniques Cary had learned in his studies with us, he began calling up the Winds to disperse the constant dense cloud of smog around the Trump Tower. So successful was he in rolling back the pollution and sometimes storm clouds that there was a peculiar clear ring of sky that would appear each day around the Trump Tower.

When Cary shared the above story with me, I jokingly referred to him as a crazy shaman who would have been arrested for witchcraft in another time period. We both had a good laugh at this.

At the same time that I was writing about Cary, I received an e-mail from him of a video he had made of what I described as a grand slam home run with the Chicago Cubs. The video Cary sent me, which accompanied his e-mail described the energy work he had begun doing for the Chicago Cubs beginning July 16, 2011. Before July 16, it stated that the win/loss record of the Chicago Cubs was thirty-nine percent. Since Cary did energy work on the team and Wrigley Field, the Cubs have won fifty-eight percent of their games. This of course is an experiment which, as I write, has not yet been completed. But if they keep up those percentages they will definitely wind up as pennant contenders instead of in the cellar. Cary's brief video describing his experience is entitled *Energy Make over Challenge.*

Sean is another apprentice who has demonstrated his soul powers. Although Sean sees me as his mentor and something of a father figure, I claim no credit for his accomplishments. I have felt the source of rapid unfolding of Astrid's abilities is the ecstatic joy she has with all life. If I were to name the source of Sean's amazing abilities, I would probably say it is his complete faith in God. Sean is an embodiment of the words of the Nazarene, "except you believe as little children . . ." It does not occur to Sean that he cannot perform miracles. In this sense Sean is truly blessed.

Although not affiliated with any church, Sean was attending a non-denominational church with a friend about a year before the writing of this chapter. After the service he felt himself drawn to a man who had been carried in by several men and placed in a chair in the back of the church. After the service Sean took the man's hands, and

163

although he had no idea what his problems were, he told him he would be able to walk. Sean was unaware that the man had never walked a day in his life. Before the astonished people who knew him, the man got out of his chair and began walking on his own around the church. As a result of the faith and courage of Sean, who had never met this man and knew nothing about him, this man's life was transformed.

Some Amazing, Off-the-Chart Feats by Colleagues, Friends and Associates

Astrid and I are friends with a "mountain man" from Virginia who, although without any higher education and with the help of others, has authored several books. He is a sought-after speaker who wears a big hunting knife to his lectures – a tough exterior with a soft, compassionate heart. One of our friend's remarkable talents is his ability to radically reduce crime and violence in troubled communities and schools.

In one ghetto school plagued by extreme violence and mass faculty resignations, by using intent and focus he reduced the incidence of violent episodes to ten percent of what it had been. Faculty attitudes have been totally transformed – all this without ever showing up at the school. This mountain man is sought after by many local school and law enforcement agencies that do not understand how he does it, but know this unusual man can deliver the goods. His great advantage over most of us is that it never occurs to him that he cannot do these things. In this way he, like Sean, is truly blessed.

When I reflect upon the accomplishments of people like those mentioned above, I am reminded of a story I once heard about a young man from India who found his master, whom he revered. He diligently followed every teaching to the letter. No master could have had a more devout follower. One day the master came to his apprentice unexpectedly and was shocked to see that he had learned to fly!
"Who taught you how to do this?" he demanded.

"Why, it was your teaching that made it possible. I thought I was supposed to fly."

"But these were not supposed to help you fly," the master said, obviously upset. At that point, the apprentice lost his ability to fly.

One of our associates loves to speak in his lectures about a friend of his who decided to see if he could live off water alone by using intention to fill the water with all the nutrients he would need. He was amazingly successful and to this day, he drinks about ten or twelve charged glasses of water and remains in excellent health.

Finally, I think of my late friend and archeologist, Pino Turolla, who while exploring in the Amazon basin, had a tragic accident in which he experienced a compound break of his right leg. It was so bad, the tibia was sticking out. To his great fortune, a group of remote tribal people discovered him. He then watched in awe as their curandero proceeded to reset the bone and fused it together, so that he could follow them on his own to their village for further treatment. This medically impossible feat that happened years ago in the Amazon jungle to a former colleague and friend of mine is yet another example of how we are not limited to physical plane laws.

Chapter 10: The Academy of "New Science"

I have a close friend and apprentice living in northeast Canada who has had an association with several brilliant but maverick scientists who refer to their work as "New Science." Many of them are geniuses who have inventions that if released to the world could clean up the pollution of the air, water and soils, if implemented on a large-scale basis. Their inventions could also raise the quality of life in many other ways for the people of Earth.

But as he explains, for now at least, they are holding onto these inventions, refusing to let them get out. He states that most of those working in New Science are extremely paranoid. According to my apprentice, one reason for the paranoia is that many of them have been approached by individuals, groups or large corporations offering large sums of money to help get the inventions to the market. However, the investors always insist on total control of the inventions.

My apprentice, a biologist, explains that his colleagues know of associates who have sold their patents or proprietary information, only to discover that their inventions are never heard of again. Most colleagues also know of individuals whose lives and those of their families have been threatened if they continue their research and development efforts.

This particular individual was partners with an American scientist who had developed formulas that, when mixed into digested waste at waste water plants, turned the waste into organic matter almost completely devoid of toxic substance. He and his partner have some idea of why the bacteria disappear from the sewage waste, but neither they nor their fellow scientists can explain what happens to heavy metals – other than that they are transmuted into non-toxic elements. In several meetings with a large technology development company staffed primarily with ex-government technical people, all scientists with only one exception did not take issue with the possibility of transmutation when referring to this apparent miracle – a concept that has always been considered rank heresy in the field of modern science.

My apprentice describes his initial enthusiasm when, in the face of heavy skepticism, a group of city officials of a large city in his area allowed the formula to be used for a period of one year to treat a portion of the sewage waste on-site using special proprietary equipment in addition to the formula. Ordinarily the waste would have to be hauled away in trucks to a landfill. The results of the test were dramatic. Just as he stated, the waste was turned into almost pure organic soil, free of chemicals, heavy metals and harmful bacteria. My apprentice was jubilant. This could get them the recognition and funding needed to get his friend's discovery out. The city officials were amazed, their original skepticism dissolved. Imagine his shock when a few weeks before the end of the one-year experiment, he was given the cryptic message that his equipment had disappeared overnight and they would not need his services. Speculation was that the company holding the hauling contract had been involved.

What I am describing in the above story seems to be a pattern that is happening all over the world that has been going on for years. Who is it that is blocking such discoveries from getting out to the public, and what possible reason would they have for this interference? Who gains from preventing such tremendous breakthroughs for the environment and for our humanity here on Earth?

My friend thinks there are several factors that may be at work. There seems to be some evidence of active suppression of further development and implementation of some technologies by government (under the guise of national security) and by companies whose economic interests would be strongly affected. In addition, he feels that many people/groups hold conscious and subconscious fears of change and may make decisions that result in uninformed suppression of new ideas and technologies. Perhaps the time for these technologies to come forth and address urgent needs is not yet here – another reflection of the need for us to open to the great truths. Implementation of new life-changing and planet-changing technologies can dramatically affect us all, and will require a clear path to implement them that will reduce/eliminate the fear and greed that seems behind the conscious and subconscious efforts limiting this implementation.

My friend spent a year traveling with other persons like him who were from other countries and also focused on new science efforts. During this time he attended meetings and gatherings where he witnessed amazing discoveries. One man, a prominent businessman from a Mediterranean country, had developed a formula that, when only a few drops were added to gasoline or jet fuel, would cause it to burn with far greater efficiency, giving out only a trace of pollution. This meant that not only was ninety-eight percent of the pollution eliminated but automobiles and planes would get far better gas mileage.

My friend also saw this man demonstrate another chemical that when mixed with fuel would make it congeal. This chemical could be injected upon a sudden impact, preventing the fuel from catching fire and exploding. The fuel could also be more safely transported in the congealed state and then transformed back to a useable state upon delivery.

Another individual whom my friend got to know was a brilliant but eccentric scientist who recently died. The death of this remarkable man was a great loss for our planet for he had developed a device that could be stuck in the ground in several places in an extremely polluted city, and within weeks it would totally clear out the pollution of the local area. Amazingly the device ran on a twelve-volt battery. I subsequently have heard about this amazing man from other sources. It seems that the key to this simple device is that it would send out a pulsation simulating the electronic wavelength of a storm cloud at the exact moment of a lightning emission from that cloud.

Another student, who had been a helicopter pilot in Vietnam, showed me a device that he developed that could destroy hydrofluoro carbons, such as Freon gases escaping from old air-conditioner units, before they ever reach the atmosphere. Upon exposure to UV the gases release chlorine free radicals, which cause so much damage to the ozone layer by reacting with ozone to form oxygen and additional free radicals. This particular apprentice's theory, which was very simple, uses the same process Mother Nature uses: bombard the dangerous gases such as Freon with a machine that produces ultraviolet rays.

Although not a member of any group of international scientists, this apprentice faced the same problem as the others: several corporations were extremely enthusiastic in funding the project but insisted on total control.

My last personal example involves a former student who purchased a new American-made automobile in the late 70s and drove with his family from Atlanta to California for vacation. To their astonishment their new car got ninety miles to the gallon. Wondering if there was a second hidden gas tank somewhere, they took it to a service center in California to check it out. To make a long story short, when the dealer called Detroit they were told this was an experimental carburetor and was not supposed to have been released, and that they had been looking all over for it. The Detroit official offered my student $5,000 to return it to them and have it replaced with a conventional carburetor – which he did.

That was more than thirty years ago! One wonders what happened to that carburetor that could get ninety miles to the gallon.

For a moment, as you consider the stories of the above individuals, I would like you to imagine living on Earth with a free, non-polluting source of energy that is available to all – and not only are you living on an Earth relatively free of air pollution, but also you belong to a species in which disease itself has become a thing of the past.

What if I were to tell you this could have been our world today except for the greed of a few powerful individuals that are part of the controlling elitist secret cabal that I have spoken of?

When the brilliant scientist Nikola Tesla came to J.P. Morgan, the wealthy industrialist who had been financing his research, with the device he developed that could be placed in the ground as a source of energy, Morgan frowned, saying something like this: "You mean anyone could use this device anywhere just by sticking it in the ground and could have all the energy they wanted at no cost?" Tesla said, "Yes, that is true!" Morgan said that he would rather run the electricity through wires so it could be measured and charged for. Morgan stated adamantly to Tesla that he wanted to make money from electricity and that his invention was unacceptable. Morgan apparently had invested heavily in the petroleum industry and wanted to go in that direction rather than tapping this universal energy.

Morgan's response was to destroy the tower Tesla had built for his research, and to confiscate all files. Consequently our species embarked on the tragic path of relying on fossil fuels for energy that brought great wealth and power to a few people and insured a future in which pollution would become our number one problem.

Royal Rife was active in his research in the earlier part of the twentieth century. He developed a new type of microscope, and discovered to his amazement that when it was adjusted to match the energetic signature of any disease, it was possible to destroy the diseased tissues in a body without harming the healthy tissues. It worked on the same principle that a wine glass will shatter when a certain frequency of sound is used while leaving everything else intact – this is known as resonant frequencies. Rife and his researchers were able to cure one hundred percent of terminal cancer patients and virtually any disease they treated.

The then president of the American Medical Association perceived the threat to the pharmaceutical industry and medical personnel if disease were to be eliminated from the planet. Consequently Rife's research and his microscope were destroyed, and he was placed in a psychiatric ward. This brilliant and amazing humanitarian died a broken man because of the greed and avarice of a few individuals associated with the medical and pharmaceutical industries, who preferred that they and their colleagues profit from the suffering of millions of people.

Chapter 11: Fourteen Keys to Your Freedom

The following is a series of Keys, which when worked with can free you from the belief systems of our time that make up the consensus reality of our culture. These keys can unlock the door to total freedom, which is the very nature of the Edenic consciousness I have described. Some of these will come easy for you, while others will be more difficult. I suggest that you work with the easy ones first. Then take the more difficult ones and work with them one at a time. Do not let yourself get discouraged, and do not see them as obstacles, but rather as pathways that can lead you to the total freedom you so ardently seek.

FIRST KEY:
Recognizing that you have been in a prison all your life.

The first key to freedom is to recognize that most likely you have been in a prison all your life, and did not know it. In fact, you believed you were free. You were told this by those who did not know better, because they too were in bondage. This is a prison without walls, but a prison nonetheless. It is a prison of the false belief systems that were imposed on you since you were a toddler – since adults first began speaking with you. This formulated your world view, a world view that is consistent with the consensus reality of our culture and one which has enslaved the people of this world. The beginning of freedom is the very first recognition that perhaps we are not really free, and that there is something terribly wrong about what you have been told about yourself, about who you are and about your world.

SECOND KEY:
Releasing all beliefs about yourself and your world.

The second key is to let go of all "beliefs" about yourself and your world. Belief systems are the enemy of true spiritual experience. Your beliefs separate you from Truth. In fact, belief is an impediment to growth. Truth is something that is experienced, not something that is accepted as a set of doctrines or dogma. When you say you believe in

God or you believe in Christ or you believe in love, you are saying in effect that you are not that. You have put up a wall between yourself and that which you profess to believe in. The highest form of belief is no belief at all.

THIRD KEY:
To accept as truth only what you resonate with.

The third key is to accept as truth only what you resonate with, not what your thinking mind tells you is true. Resonance is a "remembering" of what you already know. They key word is resonance. Resonance is not an attribute of the mind. It is an experience of your deeper awareness, of your very being. Think of harmonics. Think of a tuning fork. Think of yourself as a tuning fork of God.

FOURTH KEY:
Let your inner senses be your unfailing guide to what is real.

The fourth key is the recognition that you have both inner and outer senses. Let your inner senses be your unfailing guides to what is real. The outer senses apply to the three lower planes: the physical, the emotional and the mental. These are illusory and, therefore, our physical senses can entrap us in the illusions of the physical plane. They are illusions of material things, of emotions and feelings, and of beliefs and belief systems.

FIFTH KEY:
You are here to imprint your essence with experience.

The fifth doorway is attention to our physical sensation. Enlightenment is very closely tied in with the imprint of our essence with experience. If you are not in the here and now and you are experiencing something, there is no imprinting because your conscious awareness is somewhere else. When you are experiencing something in your physical life, and you are focused on the present place in the present moment, then your essence gets imprinted with the experience. It may be that you are just standing by a waterfall or a big, old-growth tree. You may be talking with a friend. When your mind is somewhere else, there is no imprinting, and therefore it does not become a part of who you are. You are here to imprint your essence with experience of the physical world. The greater the intensity of your experience, the greater the imprinting will be. You are an individualized expression of our Creator God and Goddess and are here to bring back something of your experience to the One Source of all life.

SIXTH KEY:
Resist control of your life and beliefs, including the subtle forms.

Always question authority! Defy convention! Resist control of your life and beliefs, including the subtle forms of control that appear to manipulate your attitudes, choices and decisions. Be the rebel, but be a rebel with a cause!

SEVENTH KEY:
Learn to act without thinking. Instead act out of a deep knowing.

Begin learning to act without thinking. Act out of a deep knowing. Every magical or extraordinary experience that happened to me in *Soul on Fire*, and things that happened to Astrid and me since the writing of that book, were the **result of acting without thought.** If I had stopped to think about things before I spoke or acted, there would have been no stories to share with you. For example, I would not have seen a ceremonial fire spontaneously combust if I had stopped to think about whether I should or should not; whether it was possible; whether it was the height of arrogance to think that I could do this? When we start thinking about something that comes from within, then we become disempowered. **Acting without**

thinking was our Original State that went back to the time when knowing and action were not separated or thought and action were not separated. You were magical beings at that time with abilities that today would seem almost incomprehensible, even to those of you who have been on a spiritual path for a number of years. At that time thought was experienced as a type of knowing.

EIGHTH KEY:

You live in a mirror world that adjusts and adapts itself to you.

Everyone who comes into your life, every experience that comes to you, everything that happens around you is somehow about you. You live in a mirror world, and so the world outside is a reflection of what is going on within. The world will always adapt and adjust itself to you.

NINTH KEY:

To realize Edenic consciousness you must shift from the mind

to the high heart, from your thinking function to your feeling nature.

To realize the Edenic consciousness within Yourself, you must shift from the mind to the high heart. The high heart is the source of your higher feelings, your higher nature – such as compassion, joy, courage, quietude, gratitude, unity, oneness and inner harmony. Much of the suffering of the world today is the result of identification with the mind. The mind creates duality. When the mind creates good, evil often slips in through the back door. The mind knows only separation! The high heart knows only unity and oneness. The real meaning of the Creation story, where we ate of the Tree of Knowledge of Good and Evil, was our fall into duality. This has been the source of much of the suffering of the world for the last 13,000 years.

TENTH KEY:
You are often entangled with other persons through past experiences

often preventing you from speaking with your true voice.

It is rightfully said "what tangled webs we weave!" Most people on this Earth are connected to many other people in their present and past through energetic threads. These threads interconnect you with people you have been in relationship with. It is an important step in your freedom to realize that you seldom speak with your own voice. By using the techniques described in this book, you will learn to cut the negative energetic threads that keep you tied to these relationships and their negative history.

ELEVENTH KEY:
Changing your perception of yourself and the world you live in

is the key to your liberation.

One of the most important keys to your freedom is changing your perceptions of how you view the world and how you view yourself. The way you see the world determines your experience of the world. You are limited to your perception of the world that the culture has impressed on you. Many of us have been radically limited in terms of what we potentially could experience. The way you perceive yourself determines the way in which you experience yourself, and it determines what you attract into your life. So changing the way you perceive yourself, and perceiving yourself as a magical being without limitations, is the beginning of freedom to express your full capacity.

TWELFTH KEY:
The majority of us carry imprints in our energy field as the

result of trauma in this life or previous lives.

We have all been incarnated in this life and previous lives with imprints from traumatic experiences. These imprints carry the emotional memory of what happened. Because of the imprints that you carry, it is difficult to act out of your own center. These programs of the past get triggered again and again, and they influence the way you act in your daily life. These imprints also serve as a type of negative magnetism that continues to attract throughout your life, and even into the next life. These are negative situations that are energetically linked to the experience of the original trauma. By using the techniques that are described in this book, you can remove these imprints, remove the energetic source, remove the foreign energy, and free yourself to act out of your center.

THIRTEENTH KEY:
Fall deeply and passionately in love with all life on Earth.

Fall deeply and passionately in love with all life on Earth, from the tiniest flower or butterfly to the great elephants and whales that sound the bass notes of our Earth. When you look into the face of a tiny child or homeless person, see in them your own reflection and that of the Infinite Creator as well.

FOURTEENTH KEY:
Recognize that our Earth is a living sentient being that

is responsible for all that you have and are.

The fourteenth key is in some ways the most important of all. It is the recognition of our Earth as the physical manifestation of the Living, Sentient Being who is responsible for all that you have and are. You should honor this Sacred Being with sacred songs, dances and ceremony. The Earth Goddess does not need to be worshipped, only acknowledged and appreciated. She only wishes what any woman wants for you: to be in relationship with her. When you surrender to your Earth Goddess, She in turn surrenders to you and gives you gifts and blessings beyond imagination.

Chapter 12: The Truth that Sets Us Free

My intention in sharing these extraordinary miracles and epiphanies has been to return to ordinary people the powers of direct experience and direct knowledge of God – powers that at one time were understood to be the entitlement of every human being.

I have intended to bear witness to the enormous possibilities that are within each of us in order to free us from limiting, suppressive and disempowering belief systems that have been imposed on us.

These belief systems, which have become our "consensus reality," are reinforced daily by the media as well as our religious, educational, political and even scientific establishments.

They are the chains that bind us and the prison walls that confine us.

They are the cause of much of the suffering in this world! That suffering will continue until we rediscover and claim that spiritual authority that is within each human being.

I was raised in a large conservative southern town in the middle of the Bible belt, where I was led to believe that the "age of miracles" ended in the first century, that the powers demonstrated by Jesus and Moses and Elijah were not available to ordinary people. Yet today I am writing about the countless miracles in my life while proclaiming that the miraculous is alive and well in all of us.

I was led to believe that one cannot have a direct experience of God except through the Church. Yet it was only after I left mainstream religion to embark on my Earth Path that I began having those ecstatic experiences and epiphanies that I had so ardently longed for.

I was led to believe that we need theologians and a professional clergy to tell us what God is like. But it was only after my "exodus" from organized religion that I came to know the Divine Source directly.

Virtually all of my most profound encounters with the Divine Presence have been not in any church, synagogue, temple, or mosque, but in the magnificent "Cathedral" of Creation!

Finally, I had been told that only the "privileged" can act with any real power in this world. But since breaking free of a prison of suppressive belief systems, I have discovered an awesome power that is available to all who truly seek it. It is the only kind of power that can never be taken from us.

In every case what those in authority told me about life's deepest truths was wrong. My freedom came from following the deepest yearnings of my heart. I discovered that the most profound truths had been inside of me all along. Like millions of others, I had been told that I was a free person and believed it, while all along living in a prison of suppressive belief systems and archaic traditions and institutions.

I learned at last not to trust authority or give up my power to the so-called experts. I finally discovered the "truth that sets us free" not in any institution or religious organization, not in any book about God, not from a religious elite and not in any building, no matter how beautiful. I found that it was inside of me all along and reflected in the marvelous Creation around me. I discovered the God/Goddess within reflected in the Creation without.

When it came time to make my leap of faith from the protective canopy of organized religion into the uncharted waters of Spirit, I could have hesitated, saying I needed to think about this, or to get a better perspective, or to do more research, or get into a better financial position, or poll the opinions of those close to me, or complain that it was not practical or not the time. If I had, I would probably still be sitting around, sinking deeper into confusion and depression.

During my ten years as a priest and priest in training in the Episcopal Church, I was haunted by the promise of Christ recorded in the Scripture: "Why are you so amazed? All these things and more shall you be able to do!" I wondered why for the last two thousand years so few had taken that promise seriously. I was struck by the realization that, whereas mainstream religions of every kind had produced devotees with great zeal, these persons seemed unable to demonstrate any real power. Indeed, many appeared to be spiritual adolescents.

Those who claimed to have had a direct experience of God so often were locked into narrow belief systems that smacked of judgment, arrogance, separatism and elitism. I felt that, if there was a God of all Creation, that God could be contained not in the narrow belief systems and ideologies I had encountered, but instead in the infinite diversity of All That Is! After years of struggle and disillusionment, I decided to claim that promise – to test its validity and find out for myself if there was any truth to it.

In the first chapter I stated that my first attempt was to administer healing on a woman in an Atlanta hospital whom I had never met. She had been given the medical sentence of death. The rest of this true-life drama is found in Soul on Fire and in this, its sequel: Life Without Limits. Whenever I attempted to test the validity of that well known but little understood promise of the Nazarene, incredible things would happen. It was as if I could not fail. I felt as if I were riding the crest of a great wave or acting out the script of a larger-than-life drama. I began having visions of the future and memories of numerous past lives. I discovered that it was possible to still a storm, as Christ once demonstrated, or to call in a storm, to invite the Winds to blow or to cease, to end prolonged drought or days of excessive rain almost immediately with strong intent and deep trust. I later learned that such things could even be done at a great distance. Perhaps most extraordinary of all: I was able to intend spontaneous combustion when preparing for fire ceremonies or in a few cases, for a type of protection or to make a point in a way that would be undeniable for those around me. In an age of great cynicism and disbelief it was sometimes necessary for me to prove that I am who I claim to be.

I also discovered that it was possible to communicate with the spirits of plants, trees and creatures of the wild; to communicate with the spirits of mountains, rivers, canyons and desert springs; in short, to enter into a conscious and ecstatic union with all of life.

Never did I perceive the extraordinary events I have described in my writings as my having power to do these things based on a whim or for self-gain or self-aggrandizement. They occurred only when I was moved by a Higher Directive or when serving a Higher Good beyond myself.

In time I began to realize that "great souls" such as **Jesus, Krishna and Buddha came not to be worshipped but to show us who we are.**

At times I have wondered if my years in the priesthood were wasted. But in retrospect I realize it was absolutely essential to know what has been lost, what needs to be retrieved, and where we have gone wrong! Otherwise how could I speak with any authority without first-hand experience? The greatest single failure of western religion today has been its refusal to address the massive environmental crisis that threatens our world. In the West we have interpreted the Biblical injunction to "have dominion over" other life forms and to "subdue the Earth" as a rationale for greed and our exploitation of our natural resources. We have polluted the oceans, the land and the air we breathe.

If there was ever a false doctrine this must be it: One subdues and conquers an enemy. In this case Earth has become our enemy! We are a species at war with the Earth. And as every aboriginal and tribal culture knows, we are a part of the Earth. Therefore, to be at war with the Earth is to be at war with ourselves. It is a war we cannot possibly win! There can be no peace ON Earth apart from peace WITH the Earth!

I would like to challenge the religious leaders and spokespersons to take the Transformational Journey themselves – not because that is what I did, but because that has been the path of virtually all of their Founders and great leaders. There is really no other way than through the Sacred Journey. Once they have undertaken that, there will be nothing left to "fix." Religion will transform because its leaders have transformed and as in the "days of old," the Light of Truth once more will stream in.

Life Without Limits is really about two of the greatest secrets of the Universe – secrets that can free us from our prisons and bring everlasting joy. First, change the way you perceive the world and the world adjusts and adapts itself according to your perceptions. If you see the world as the cold, impersonal, mechanistic universe, as many do, then that is what it reflects back to you. But, if you see it as a magical, holy place that is the embodiment of a Great and Sacred Being, a Being who loves you as a mother loves a child and is responsible for all that you have and are – then that is exactly what you will experience. Second: Try to change the way you perceive yourself, not as that wretched "fallen" being that is the subject of much of the religious dogma in the West, but as a magical being in a magical world – a divine, light-infused being for whom all things ultimately are possible.

Today we must make an "exodus" from the limiting beliefs of the past into the Promised Land of Spirit within ourselves. The key in both the above cases lies in perception. It is the key to the Kingdom of Heaven. The above secrets are the essence of my "work."

There will come a time later in this century when people will find the stories in Life Without Limits unremarkable, because many will be demonstrating their own soul powers in the years ahead. At first there will be just a few, then a hundred, and at some point after that a critical mass is achieved. When that happens, a change in our entire species occurs at the quantum level, in the DNA itself, and the experiences I have written about will be commonplace.

It has been my intention to prove the Truth of Jesus' Great Promise and implicitly the teachings of all the Masters, that we shall be able to manifest the marvelous gifts of Spirit – our inherent Soul Powers. I believe that I have succeeded in doing this.

Many who have read Life Without Limits as well as my earlier book, Soul on Fire, have found the stories remarkable. But for a number of people the stories have struck a chord. Something in them resonates deeply with the unusual experiences I have described. That resonance is a bodily remembering of who they truly are. Such remembrance takes place on a level much deeper than the mind can penetrate. It is with such remembering that the awakening of Soul Powers occurs. These two books are my "wake-up call" for those people who are ready to manifest their Soul Powers.

My challenge to you is this: Do you dare to speak your truth?

As soon as you say, "I can do this," it becomes possible! The moment you make the claim that you can manifest this power, then that power is available to you.

Our culture has disempowered us with labels of arrogance or egotism whenever we think or step outside of the box. But when we publicly claim our power as divine Beings, it is not arrogance but entitlement, not egotism but empowerment.

All this takes courage! The doubting Thomas in us questions, "What if I fail?" and the ego asks, "What if I make a fool of myself?"

Can you imagine how the conventional side of me felt when I heard myself saying: "I can heal this person of cancer!" or manifest spontaneous combustion in a fire ceremony to end a two-and-a-half year drought, or to clear pollution out of a thirty-mile radius for two weeks at a time, or bring back a long vanished species to the Smoky Mountains? Even though that conventional part of me has never quite died, I have consistently refused to give it any power.

Years ago I was speaking to a group of graduate students and faculty of a Presbyterian Seminary. While some were supportive, others were defensive and argumentative. Finally, an African graduate student said to me, "You are different from the others I have met over here. You speak with – what is the word? Certitude! You speak with such certitude!" How many of our religious leaders are able to speak with the certitude that comes from direct experience and knowledge of the Divine?

When any one of us speaks our Truth that comes not from the mind, but from the center of being, there is no room for argument or debate. There is only Truth!

When we do this, it gives others courage to do it. When we demonstrate of our Soul Powers, it empowers others to demonstrate the truths about who we really are.

Many Christians look for the return of the Christ to make things right, while the Jews still await the coming of their Messiah; a number of New Age people expect the extraterrestrials to come and set things right; while many of the Native People of our land like the

Hopi anticipate the return of the Kachinas, who are sacred beings from the stars. There is a Hopi prophecy that when the time is ripe, when humans have forgotten who they are, forgotten their connection with the Source, when there is violence and oppression everywhere, and the Earth Herself is dying – it is then that the Kachinas, or Star Beings, will return and restore all things. Similar prophecies are found in ancient cultures throughout the world.

I suspect that if we are to survive this twenty-first century, our salvation will come from those of us who have chosen to be a part of this Earth Walk in the present time. Amazingly, a few years ago some of the Hopi elders came to the same startling realization. They stated that the Kachinas are already here, and those sacred beings from the stars are us! In other words, they now insist that we do not have to continue to look outside of ourselves for our deliverance.

We are that deliverance. We are the ones we have been waiting for!

Chapter 13: Summary

In my first book, *Soul on Fire*, I shared a number of stories of magical yet true experiences from my own spiritual journey. I hoped they would provide cumulative evidence in support of the truth that we are creatures who are in no way limited to the laws of the physical plane; that we are far more than we were led to believe by our mentors when we were growing up; and that who we are cannot be defined by the consensus reality of our culture.

In relating these stories, although they were accurate down to the detail, I used some literary license by playing the role of being amazed by my ability to effect events that are beyond the laws of the physical plane. In reality I did have a sense of who I was and of my own abilities. One could say that there were at least two selves involved; there was the "young" self – plagued with doubts, uncertainties, and skepticism, and being threatened about the magic that was occurring; and there was an older, wise self who fully understood what was happening. I knowingly put myself on the spot again and again, when I would call in a storm, spontaneously combust ceremonial fires, tell my students we would see a bear at a certain time of day in a specific location, or state that I would bring in instant healing to someone who had damaged his larynx in an automobile accident.

For those students who remained in their head, there was no real magic. For them Astrid and I were little more than magicians pulling rabbits out of hats. They would say: "I **saw** Peter combust a ceremonial fire or call in a thunderstorm." "I **saw** Astrid call different species out of the forest." "I **saw** her stop a wind blowing a forest fire down a canyon." Yet they missed the point, because only their minds were titillated. However, those who had shifted to their body-mind and their feeling nature had profound experiences.

It is important to remember that we could not have demonstrated any of the powers I have described if we were coming out of our heads. It would have been impossible! There is no spiritual power in the mind, which is not a function of our true essence. In every instance, whenever some magical event occurred, Astrid and I were coming out of our heart/solar plexus/feeling nature. The solar plexus, in fact, is the location of the body-mind, which connects us to our cellular consciousness and to all life around us. We must be "in the body," not the head, to perform the magic described in this book. Likewise, our students and apprentices needed to be in that same space, which is to be in the present moment.

√ The solar plexus is our primitive brain. When we operated out of that chakra, we were connected to the Earth and Sky, the Fire and Wind, the spirit of the trees, the plants and the rocks. We were always in the present moment and knew no separation. With the development of the rational mind (cerebral cortex), mankind became separated from the feeling nature and the "oneness" we had known. Now is the time to regain what has been lost. It is time for a shift into a fifth dimensional world. That is why I feel such urgency about what must be achieved. There was a touch of pathos here. Those who made the shift that I have described, thrived. Those who did not were left behind. This is a microcosm of what will be happening in our world in the decades ahead. Not all will "get it." Those who do not will have to await a large span of time before such an opportunity comes around again.

In *Life Without Limits*, I have spoken directly, proclaiming the great hidden truth of who we really are: beings without limitations of any kind.

I have given numerous examples to support this radical and revolutionary concept. It is said that **revolutionary new ideas always follow the pattern of initial ridicule, then anger and finally acceptance**.

Those examples span a wide diversity of our experiences on Earth. I have cited numerous examples from my own life, that of my partner Astrid, and a few of our apprentices. That some of us have been able to experience and demonstrate, at will, some of these powers begs the question: If the above is a true reflection of who we are, then why are most of us leading lives that are so limited and ineffectual by comparison? What occurred that disempowered so many of us? I suggest that it is a case of deliberate deception and rampant ignorance, combined with our blind and unquestioning acceptance of what we have been told about our world and who we are.

When I first realized that we are truly beings without limitations, I assumed this discovery would come as a welcome message of liberation for those who heard it. I believed it would be joyously received and open many hearts and minds, as it did for Astrid and me. To my surprise, there was a mixed response. Some did not wish to hear that they could have done better. Others saw this as a judgment of the way they had lived their lives. Still others simply did not want to change their lives.

This came as a shock to me, shattering my idealism about human nature. After my bubble had burst, I began to sense the urgency, more than ever, of getting these ideas out. I realized that acceptance by even a small minority of the human inhabitants on this planet would bring about a global transformation.

There is a little-known truth that goes like this: **In most periods of Earth history when there is relative stability, an enormous effort is required by a large number of people to bring about a major paradigm shift. But if the world is moving into a period of great instability or chaos, as it is today, with our planet and the human species spiraling toward destruction, it takes only a small minority of people to bring about a major change. As never before in the history of our world, we have the opportunity to usher in a veritable utopia – a new Eden that would be a paradise on Earth. I feel great passion for this message I have been asked to deliver to all who will listen.**

Now is the time in Earth history in which at last we can let go of our limiting beliefs that have disempowered us for so many lifetimes. We can release the crippling judgments about ourselves and others and the weightiness of our regrets and guilt that keep us Earthbound.

We no longer need to live in this **fear-based society** or get trapped in the **survival mentality** that has infected our species like a deadly virus. Nor do we have to be victims to a small, elitist group that, in their own way, are just as stuck as we are and are to be pitied. It is time to say: "Enough is enough – we no longer wish to be

197

victimized, nor do we wish to continue playing the game of separation."

A utopia awaits us; an Earthly paradise is in the offing! We must make conscious choices to break out of this prison without walls.

 "A great vision is needed, and he who has it must follow it, as the eagle seeks the deepest blue of the sky." – Chief Crazy Horse, 1840-1877.

 "I salute the light within your eyes where the whole universe dwells."
– Chief Crazy Horse.

Epilogue

A Kaleidoscope of Images

As I come to the close of this book I am aware that it marks the completion of a certain phase of my life – the part in which at last, after four decades, I am getting my ideas out. The teachings are based on a **direct experience** of our Infinite Creator, not the general approach in the West for the past two thousand years which is that we can only experience and know God indirectly through a mediator, such as the church, a clergy, the saints, Mary, or Jesus himself. As sovereign spiritual and immortal Beings, all of us can open to this direct experience. How is it that we in need of being saved? Saved from what or from whom? Do we not all go on forever?

Once we have connected to the deep intuitive faculties of the heart, we no longer need to be told what is right or what to do. This knowledge is open to all of us, from the most exalted to the most humble.

At this moment a kaleidoscope of images continually shifts before me – images that reflect different significant and luminous moments of my Life's Journey. I see before me verdant forest – the majestic mountain peaks of the Grand Tetons of Wyoming, the white faced cliffs of the Blue Ridge Mountains of North Carolina. I see numerous waterfalls, cascading streams and alpine lakes mirroring bright clouds and the surrounding snow capped mountains.

Then there are the changing patterns of sunlight reflected off the red rock canyon walls of Utah and Arizona, large cottonwood trees that provide welcome protection from the intense sunlight of the Southwest.

Now I hear the elemental sounds of running water, wind and distant thunder.

John Muir, the great naturalist of the eighteenth century, once was asked what stood out most in his memories of his amazing months' long trek across the Americas. Without hesitation, he replied: "Wind." It was the sound of the wind in the trees, through the canyons and over the grasslands.

And how could I not remember the wonderful sounds of the winged messengers that would herald the dawn or usher in nightfall.

I remember well the chorus of coyotes breaking the silence of the desert night, the bugling of bull elks in the fall, and other sounds I could not quite identify, like the sounds of wind and water. These sounds were music to my ears.

Especially powerful are the memories evoked by the many deer, elk, bears, coyotes and cougars, that played powerful roles in the unfolding dramas of Astrid's and my journey.

I cannot fail to speak of the fragrances of new growth of pine, of honeysuckle, azalea and sweet scrub in the southern mountains at springtime. It is said that the olfactory sense is the oldest in our evolution and is closely associated with memories of past experiences. I believe this to be true.

Now at seventy-five, as I am approaching a time of completion of what I set out to achieve, I feel many different emotions welling up inside me. I see many of Earth's wild creatures passing in review. These are the wonderful Beings – emissaries of our Earth Goddess that played such important roles in Astrid's and my development. What wonderful friends and teachers they were. What special moments of joy they provided.

Finally I see the faces of those I loved and who loved me as we shared this unforgettable journey. There is first of all my twin soul, Astrid, so filled with wisdom and childlike wonder, joy and laughter. Her "light touch" and her ability to always "lighten up" provided a perfect balance for me. There were numerous others whose support in other ways was beyond measure. Were it not for these people, I would not be delivering the message contained in this text. There were both my human friends and all those wondrous Nature and Earth spirits that taught me so much.

These are some of the impressions I receive that are part of the "imprinting" of my essence with experience of the world around me. These memories then become more than memories. They become part of who I am and, unlike most experiences, are indelibly imprinted for all time and eternity in my soul essence.

The Rise and Fall of Atlantis

A Forthcoming Book by Peter

It is one of my first time travels! The emotional intensity of this experience is beyond that of lucid dreaming and most waking experiences: I am standing in a large circular temple beneath a huge faceted crystal that is placed in the dome overhead. The force field of this crystal is enormously powerful and slightly unnerving. Throughout the following day I am still able to feel this force field.

Suspended presumably by the power of the crystal about four feet above the floor is an open book containing glyphs similar to those of ancient Egypt, but which are definitely not Egyptian. Prior to this time travel, I never consciously believed in the existence of the Lost Continent, but as I stand in the temple, I know the glyphs are Atlantean, and to my surprise I am able to read them. The pages are made of an unknown substance that enables me to read the entire book without turning any pages.

I feel a sense of urgency! There is danger here! There are powerful, highly negative people who are seeking to get possession of this book and use the knowledge it contains for the wrong purpose. Already they have gained control of much of Atlantis and many of the people. Their access to this book could further endanger Atlantis and bring great destruction to the land itself. This book of scientific and psychic law is entitled simply the *Book of One*. It was brought to Atlantis thousands of years earlier by beings of another galaxy to help the Atlanteans and prevent them from the misuse of energy and power which had destroyed their own world of Arkadia.

It was this book that enabled the Atlanteans to create a veritable utopia that existed for thousands of years. During this entire time it had been protected in the central temple of Atlantis, The Temple of One. This central temple, of which I was the High Priest or Custodian, was surrounded by twelve other temples, each presided over by a high priest.

It appears that, because of the nature of my position as guardian and interpreter of this sacred book, I had been allowed to remain on Atlantis for an extraordinarily long period of time. In the greatly heightened state of awareness that I experienced during this time travel, I knew that long ago disease had been conquered, and also that the aging process could be reversed with the crystal technology (the legendary Fountain of Youth?). Consequently people did not ordinarily die of old age or disease. They were allowed to remain on Atlantis for one hundred, two hundred, or three hundred revolutions of the sun, depending on their contributions to the culture.

In this land people appeared to move from one place to another simply by willing it. Their disc-shaped craft containing a large faceted crystal that was charged with the rays of the sun and programmed with the mind was a means of traveling beyond this world. I was aware by direct knowledge that in the past there had been an exploration not only of our galaxy but of the far reaches of the universe.

The Atlanteans had used the temples as places of learning, healing and numerous other purposes. Children were taught methods of healing, bilocation, astral projection and teleportation, much as children today are taught the three R's.

The Temple of One was the center of training for advanced initiates. It was where those training to be priests studied and contemplated the contents of the *Book of One*.

Accompanying me in the temple was Enor, a temple priest. Because of the dark ones we had made the reluctant decision to destroy the *Book of One* by the elemental force of Fire. Both of us were feeling a deep sense of pathos over that which we were about to do. So much good could have been accomplished by this book as it had in the past. In hopes that the *Book of One* could be brought back at a much later time, we had decided to commit it to our memory so that it would become part of our permanent Akashic records.

Significantly, this time travel went to the exact time that I was committing the *Book of One* to memory. This process involved reading one page at a time, then turning away and repeating the contents to myself. I would then move on to the next page repeating the process, always checking to be sure that it was indeed a part of my memory. We also knew that our lives were in immediate and grave danger. It was only a matter of a brief time before we would be apprehended. We had made the decision to permanently leave the body, since the dark ones would be able to scan our memories if we were apprehended.

For days after my time travel to Atlantis, I pondered this experience of reliving part of a past life that occurred 30,000 years ago. This was shortly before the second of three destructions of the land mass of Atlantis. Atlantis was still a large continent, but following the second destruction only a few islands remained of the large land mass.

We now know that the final destruction of Atlantis occurred approximately 12,000 years ago, when Atlantis once again was a place of great scientific and technological advancement. Our science and technology of today are but rudiments of what existed during those great periods of light.

What happened during that vast period of time between these two cultures? Did the world plunge back into a stone age? Were there ice ages? Or was much of the science and technology preserved after the colossal second destruction? If one considers the nature of the great cycles of our Earth, including the 26,000 year precession of the equinox, then we are led to believe that so much was lost 30,000 years ago that our species had to start all over again.

It was two weeks after my time travel to Atlantis that I received a letter that profoundly changed my life and the way I viewed our world today. The letter was from a woman who had heard me speak at an Edgar Cayce study group. She wrote: "Peter, the other night I asked God to give me a dream of a past life important to me. Two nights in a row I had the same exact dream in which you and I were in Atlantis. I had never believed in the existence of the Lost Continent, but in this dream people seemed very advanced. They were able to move about from one place to another without visible means of travel. You and I were concerned with the safety of a book. In that dream we ended up destroying it by the element of Fire which we seemed able to just will into manifestation. Cordially, Evelyn."

I found myself shaking uncontrollably while reading Evelyn's letter. Perhaps it was a bodily response to the enormity of the information we would be uncovering in the weeks ahead. During the year that followed we met regularly to recover more of the contents of this book that belonged to another age in the distant past. I would be learning much more about the forces which brought about the emergence of this forgotten civilization. My life was about to change dramatically, and I could feel it in every cell in my body.

The experience I described raised many questions: 1) Who were the Atlanteans, 2) what were their achievements, 3) what led to their demise, 4) is America the new Atlantis, 5) are we faced with the same problems and choices the Atlanteans were faced with, 6) do we have to get it right this time, (7) what kind of book was it that these dark people were obsessed with getting their hands on, (8) why did it have to be destroyed, (9) who were the Arkadians, (10) what did they have to teach us, (11) would it be possible to extract information contained in the *Book of One* that would be helpful to us in the present?

These were riddles I attempted to unravel during the next year as Evelyn and I extracted the contents of the Atlantean book of scientific and psychic law.

I will now share the introduction to the *Book of One* and another passage from it for you to see if you resonate with what it says.

Introduction to the *Book of One*

"There is nothing more and nothing less than the Absolute. The whole Creation is the Absolute manifesting in different forms and densities.

The creature Man has been given the gift of potential awareness of his place in the One. No one has a right to such a gift and, as with any gift, it can be taken away. The paths, methods and techniques in this book are for the purpose of attaining Oneness. Any misuse of this knowledge can lead to a drastic setback in the development of one's consciousness. The reader here is solemnly advised that whatever information he shares with any other, he shares that person's responsibility. Man, when he begins to become aware of the almost unlimited powers within him, tends to run too fast, stumbling over his own steps in the process. The whole Creation is continually calling Itself to Itself. It calls; it does not demand."

I was intrigued to learn of a prophecy attributed to the High Priest, Meldor, that was attached to the *Book of One*. That prophecy described a time in the far distant future when the *Book of One* would be given back. According to that prophecy **that time is now:**

"The *Book of One* will be given back some day in the far, far distant future. It will be at a time of small and great wars, a time when people once again seek to control not just situations but other people; a time when people become so attached to the material that they become like things themselves, closing out positive force. It will be at a time of great scientific and technological breakthroughs and great new revelations in the spiritual nature of Man. It will be in an age in the far, far distant future, an age so-called Aquarius."

To be continued in my forthcoming book on the Lost Continent and the Book of One.

Self-Help Exercises:

I. Non-Ordinary Wisdom

Below are insights, mostly my own inspiration, based on my personal struggles in the school of hard knocks. Can you relate to any of these?

Live in the moment, not for the moment.

Be attached to nothing and nothing can be taken away from you.

When effort turns to struggle, you have already lost.

You will not find love by seeking love. If you are seeking love, it will elude you or you will attract another needing love. When you remember you are love, then you will draw to yourself the love of your life.

Doing requires energy; being returns energy to you.

We cannot *have* peace on Earth until we have *made* peace with Earth.

We cannot have "good will toward men" apart from good will toward all life.

Much can be gained from effort; more can be achieved through the effortless effort.

We are not a part of the Whole; we are that Whole. ⭝

Enlightenment is not a drop of water falling into the ocean; it is the ocean poured into that drop of water. ⭝

To always do what others want of you is the ultimate betrayal of self.

"Do that which best serves you, and all others will best be served." *Conservations with Goa*, Neale Donald Walsch.

To defend your position requires much energy; to have no castle walls to defend frees up energy and returns it to us.

Why be a truth seeker? When one seeks that which is outside of self, it can elude you. Instead remember that you are truth and become a living embodiment of that truth.

Abundance is not something to get, it is not outside of you. You are abundance; therefore, simply call it forth into manifestation.

Try eliminating the violence toward life in our figures of speech. We need to stop speaking about "killing time," "taking up space," our "conquest of Nature," "taming the frontier," and we need to remove our bible verses that talk about subduing the Earth and having dominion over all forms of life.

The mind always creates duality. When the mind attempts to create good, evil often comes in by the back door.

There can be no freedom under the "tyranny of time" – no liberation while caught in the madness of the mind.

What the mind must believe in, the heart already knows.

Learn to surrender without giving up, to let go without giving in.

Belief impedes growth; it sets up the conditions for separation, judgment and divisiveness. The highest form of belief is no belief.

"It is better to become Christ than it is to believe in him." – Maharshi

The flip side of divine compassion is divine detachment; both are necessary.

To be detached is freedom, to be disconnected leads to isolation.

"Enlightenment is to lighten up." – The Dali Lama

"Enlightenment is waking up." – Buddha

"Enlightenment is the end of suffering." – Buddha
Enlightenment is remembering who and what you are.

"Emptiness is the ultimate expression of reality." – The Dali Lama

Say yes to empowerment, no to power over. Empowerment is liberation; power over leads to entrapment.

To need repels; to be in a state of magnetic attraction draws all that you require to yourself.

To never surrender is a recipe to being brought to one's knees.

The restless winds of the mind stir up the ocean of emotion; once stirred up, to hold back emotion is like holding back the ocean. Who would succeed in that? Better to control the trigger for those emotions, which are your thoughts.

II. Exercises and Techniques

The following methods will enable you to perform some of the remarkable activities Astrid and I have been able to accomplish. Some of these are described in my book *Soul on Fire*. These methods include placing an energetic boundary around your garden that will completely protect it from invasion, making a contractual agreement with a species, communicating with your animal companions including the wild creatures of your area, going into a natural area and being accepted by all its inhabitants, and reading the invisible landscape around you.

1. Communicating with your animal companions

    Stop the internal chatter of your mind. If you are unable to do this, simply observe your thoughts or your breath without identifying with them.

    Allow yourself, without forcing the issue, to be in the present ever-expanding moment.

    Shift from your thinking function to your feeling nature. This is a shift from the mind to the heart.

    Speak softly to your animal friends, even if they are not in sight, explaining what you wish them to do or what you desire to do for them, while at the same time sending appropriate images. Remember, pictures are the universal mode of communication.

    Send love along with feelings of gratitude and appreciation.

    Wait and see what happens.

2. Making a "deal" or contractual agreement for a win-win situation

    • If you are having a problem with a species of animal, bird, reptile or insect that has invaded your home or property, try connecting with them in the way described above.

    Explain that they are in the wrong place and that it could be harmful for them to stay; that you do not wish them to be hurt.

    If possible, suggest another place that would be more suitable.

Remember to speak aloud because your voice helps you to focus but it is your specific images and feelings that reach your animal companions.

3. No longer an "exile" in the garden of the natural world

First, pay close attention to how Nature grows silent when you enter – that is because the energy of your conscious mind and thoughts is alien to all creatures of the wild; they feel threatened.

Now having quieted your mind and shifted to your feeling nature, walk into the same natural area remembering to be present with yourself.

Remember that it is our appreciation of the animals, plants, trees and rocks that enables them to realize their own specialness and become self-aware.

Pay attention to how, for the first time, the world of Nature does not grow silent when you enter. You have now been accepted as part of the environment.

Remain quiet for some time, noting how the animals no longer fear you.

In time you may be able to approach and even mingle with the larger animals without their running away.

4. Placing an energetic dome over your garden

To protect your garden from invasion of wild creatures, visualize and state your intention that your garden be protected from invasion by animals, birds or insects.

At the same time, place an "energetic dome" over your garden and visualize it keeping all intruders out.

Request the assistance of the Nature elementals in your area, promising that in exchange you will leave a portion of your bounty each week outside your garden for the creatures. Also you might wish to create a small wild area for the small animals. These latter two steps are for you to honor the universal law of exchange that says, whenever we ask for something, we give something back in return that is of equal or greater value. You will be amazed at the results.

5. Reading the invisible landscape of a natural area

- This requires some practice, but the rewards are great. Walk into a natural area using the disciplines described above.

- Begin paying attention and take note of any picture in your mind that might pertain to the recent history or the present activities of the area.

- Note any bodily sensations. The body is a tuning fork that resonates with the sudden shifts of your inner being. It is another way of "seeing." Remember this: The mind can deceive, but the body is incapable of deception or of being deceived. It is your "tuning fork" of the soul.

- Pay attention to any feeling of concentric rings that might reflect any life forms in your area, or the recent history of the place, as well as the presence of animals, humans or Nature spirits. Such events in the world of Nature can be likened to stones dropped in a pool of water, but in this case you are immersed in the ocean of radiant energy sending out ripples that we call concentric rings.

- Pay attention to any "imprint" that might reflect a violent event of the past. A person who was injured, a hunter that shot a deer, even a hawk that catches a tiny field mouse will imprint an area much like that of a photographic film.

Strategies for Connecting with the Beings and Energies of the Invisible World Around Us

1. Events come in sideways. (This is more of a metaphorical than a literal concept.)

2. Use peripheral vision or blurred vision rather than direct vision. When you look at something not of this dimension, it eludes you.

3. Ears and eyes should be unfocused. Do not single out individual sounds and sights – this is sometimes called soft eyes.

4. Be childlike in your approach. Approach each experience as if for the first time. This is known as the beginner's mind. Be totally present with this experience, joyous and spontaneous.

5. Use the power of what I call indirect observation. Learn to watch and not watch at the same time, because to focus

directly in an attempt to get information will usually push it away.

6. Be detached with no investment in the outcome.
7. Let go of the need to get results.
8. Be without effort. In this case, effort will work against you.

Did you notice the difference?

The birds and squirrels will tell you when you are able to blend in vibrationally and are no longer an outsider. You are no longer in exile in the Garden of Eden.

Changing Perceptions

1. Spend a day alone without TV, radio, stereo, cell phone, computer or newspapers. Work solely with your spiritual practices.

2. Now go to a public area such as a shopping center, imagining you are from another world, visiting Earth for the first time. Observe the faces and mannerisms of these Earth people. Notice the quality and resonance of their voices, their topics of conversation. What do you conclude? What effect do the people have on you?

Reading the Invisible Landscape

The energetic world around us is far older and more complex than our physical world. Its energies and the beings inhabiting it influence our realities in numerous ways. Now practice the shaman's gait when you are out in Nature and open yourself to Nature's energies. When you ask for assistance from the beings of the energetic world, always make an offering in return. Remember also to express gratitude, avoiding the error of seeing yourself as apart from or different from them. You are one and yet separate from them, with different functions.

Concentric Rings, Vortices, Imprints and Magnetic Fields

Using techniques you have learned, activate your field of energy and begin your walk. Monitor all changes in the field around you, noting any fleeting images of animals or activities in your immediate area. Feel any boundaries you pass through, make note of any anomalies in the energy field, and note any presences, disturbances, spirit activity or what you sense about the recent history of the area you are visiting.

Finding Your Soul Purpose

Your goals in life, such as being successful in business, acquiring your dream home or visiting beautiful places, are not a part of your life purpose; those are the things, noble or practical as they may be, that you aspire to. What do you think you came here to accomplish? What is the driving, compelling urge in your life? The answers to these questions should give you a sense of your soul purpose. Is it to heal, to guide, to serve others, to take care of others or the animals, to create beauty? These would be part of your soul purpose.

Neutralizing Repetitive Patterns of the Past

I refer to the above exercises and techniques as canceling Groundhog Day in reference to the popular movie starring Bill Murray. Buddha called repetitive patterns the law of recurrence, saying that this rather than karma is the greatest problem for humans on this Earth. What patterns have you brought into this life such as poverty consciousness, low self-esteem, victim consciousness, a tendency to judge yourself or others, being unable to finish a task or start one? What are the inexplicable fears in your life such as of water, heights, failure, being alone, rejection, intimacy? These are the repetitive patterns that have haunted you, lifetime after lifetime, and will continue until they are recognized and neutralized.

Exercise: Using the following method of neutralizing karma and false beliefs, attempt to neutralize these negative patterns that have haunted you.

Detecting and neutralizing your false beliefs

1. Make a list of the limiting and therefore false beliefs you have had about yourself and your world. Include the more unconscious limiting beliefs that may go back to childhood or even a past life, such as belief in scarcity, lack, or never enough love, money or time.
2. Using the following threefold method, neutralize the limiting belief. (When necessary you may wish to state your forgiveness for self and your mentors for embracing this false truth.)
   Visualization
   Feeling
   Replacing with a higher truth.

Recapitulation

1. Do a recapitulation of your life, always beginning with the present and working backward.
2. When you come to a person or experience that carries an emotional charge, either positive or negative, hold that person or yourself in your awareness, stating forgiveness, if necessary, and your intent to transmute all residual feelings and emotions surrounding that experience.
3. Hold the above visualization and memory until you feel a lifting off or dissolving of the weight of the emotion. (Remember also that a positive emotion can cause us to yearn for the past and pull us out of the present, such as a longing to be somewhere else or with someone else or to repeat a certain experience). Take several hours to do the

above, working only with what surfaces at the time. Do not attempt to remember everything,

4. Now do you feel lighter, freer and more expansive? If so, you have done your work.

III. Thinking Outside the Box

Below is a series of situations that can help you to stretch your mind. These are not hypothetical. They are actual situations that Astrid or I have faced, in which we had to think outside the box in order to resolve them. Please attempt to come up with your own solution before checking Section IV for the way we dealt with each situation. You will see that there are no correct answers. Have fun!

1. A car is riding your bumper; the driver guns it, screaming at you as he passes, then swerves in front of you, nearly forcing you off the road. How do you respond?

2. Describe how you would find a power spot. What would you avoid?

3. You are considering moving to another area and are drawn to several different places. As a modern-day shaman, how would you choose?

4. What would indicate to you that a place might have "bad medicine" connected to it?

5. How can you determine if an encounter or sighting in Nature is truly a sign?

6. What do you feel is missing in the approach of many persons engaged in Nature sports such as rock climbing, mountain climbing and even many hiking clubs?

7. You wish to clear a home or land of "bad medicine." Whom would you call on from the subtle realms for assistance?

8. The drum is sometimes called "the shaman's horse." What does this mean?

9. Describe how you would read the invisible landscape when you are exploring the natural world. Can you think of an example when you have done this?

10. What do you think is meant by the terms concentric rings, magnetic fields, energy vortices, grids, grid lines, imprints and subtle shifts in energy?

11. What do think is meant by a place where "the Four Directions come together" (or Four Winds)? What would it feel like? Why is this considered a special blessing?

12. Each of us has come in with an affinity to a specific direction (or wind). Do you sense yours? How would you find it?

13. Most of us have a particular direction we tend to avoid. For example one who has difficulty being alone would naturally avoid or fear the West, which is the place of inwardness and reflection. Do you know which direction you tend to avoid? Why is it said that our greatest power can come from working with that direction?

14. What is meant by the statement: Meditate or you disintegrate?

15. What is meant by the statement: "To access information by way of the Third Eye, you must learn to watch and not watch" at the same time?

16. The Third Eye, which exists in superposition to our physical body, is a magnetic field by which we can access information anywhere in the universe or from any point in the past or future. Why is it so rare that our species is able to use it in this way?

17. What is considered the most powerful time in the diurnal cycle?

18. What is the best time for drawing close to the inner world?

19. What is the best time span for initiating or setting something in motion?

20. Besides the solstices and equinoxes, can you think of four other times in the year that are considered by some traditions to be equally powerful?

21. When is it wise not to perform a sacred ceremony?

22. What do you think are the most evolved members of the mineral, plant and animal kingdoms? Have any achieved enlightenment?

23. Can you give three things that the use of fragrances and "smokes" could aid you in performing your sacred ceremonies?

24. Can you list six activities (or non-activities) that can assist you in stopping the internal dialogs?

25. What is the best element(s) to bring about personal changes or alter the outcome of a situation such as a court case, business dealings or personal conflict?

26. What element can best bring clarity and insight into your life?

27. What is the best place(s) to be in direct contact with the Earth Mother?

28. What is the best place(s) in Nature to perform a ceremony for manifestation?

29. What is the best element for letting go of a relationship, old habits?

30. What is generally the best setting to do a Vision Quest?

31. When you are in the outdoors and being annoyed and distracted by biting insects, what is an attitude or shift in consciousness that can free you from these very real distractions?

32. You are in a forest or mountainous area and feel a sudden interruption in the flow of things. How do you determine what it is that has caused this?

33. You are hiking in a beautiful backcountry area, and suddenly hit a "wall" and cannot go any further. You begin experiencing a primal fear that has no rational basis. What do you do?

34. You have an animal sighting while walking in a field or wooded area. How do you know if it is a sign?

35. You are anxious to begin certain spiritual practices but also need to get into some kind of "fitness" program. There is not enough time for both. How do you choose?

36. You have a disturbing dream or premonition about a friend's safety but cannot get any details regarding what it means. What are your options?

37. You have a client who has feelings of "not me" or as if a part of them were missing. What are the possible sources of these feelings and how might you assist?

38. You have a client who becomes hysterical when some previous trauma from childhood (or a past life) erupts. You have to act fast. What do you do?

39. You are camping in the dry West and awaken to a forest fire being propelled by a strong wind down a canyon towards you. You are without transportation. What are your options as a shaman?

40. You discover that your area is in the direct path of a hurricane or tornado and feel guided to intervene, in spite of your very human doubts as to whether you can make a difference. What would you seek to do? What would you wish to avoid, should you choose to intervene?

41. How would you design a hospital room or a room in your home that offers shapes, colors, etc. most conducive for healing?

42. You have been asked to provide healing to someone who appears to be possessed. How do you know whether the issue is psychic of psychotic?

43. A friend requests your aid in finding their lost dog or cat. How could you assist them?

44. How would you walk into a forest and read the etheric imprints of who lives there and where?

45. A neighbor's cats are ravaging the birds and lizards of your area. You talk to them but they will not listen. What other options do you have?

46. A client is having a string of "bad luck" episodes in his life. What are the possible sources and what could you do to intervene?

47. You are driving on a seldom traveled road and discover that a car has run off the road into a field. The driver appears to be in a coma, but not visibly injured. As a shaman you know there is a very real danger of moving this person to a hospital. What is that danger? And how would you attempt to help the injured person?

48. You are going through the process of ending a long-term relationship and you are grieving. A client or friend contacts you, informing you that they are under some kind of psychic attack and they need your help. How do you respond?

49. You are seeking to make a major move to another town or part of the country. How do you determine if a particular place is right for you (from a shamanic point of view)?

50. What is so bad about the traditional siren on ambulances and fire engines?

51. What are some indications (like birds and planes falling out of the sky) that a place might have "bad medicine?"

52. What information would you want to access to remove the bad medicine?

53. In releasing lost, wandering or negative spirits, what information would be helpful?

54. What are "elemental" attachments, what do they usually need, and how would you classify them?
55. How would you determine which kind of elemental you are dealing with, and how would you assist each kind?

56. Under what conditions might you choose to absorb a negative energy instead of warding it off or stating your desire that it be "transmuted in the healing light of God?"

57. Why do you believe that so many Hebrew, East Indian and Tibetan words are used in ceremonies, mantras and incantations? Why not stick to your own language? And why are they spoken aloud or intoned?

58. What do you think would be the limitations of the English language in communicating the higher truths?

59. Why do you think Astrid and I insist on your verbalizing such things as "intention" or "forgiveness" or "expressions of gratitude?"

60. What are the calming inward colors that can be used in therapy, the warm energetic or extraverted colors, the balancing color?

61. When would green never be used?

62. When should reds and oranges be avoided?

63. Which is the only gemstone that cannot hold a negative charge?

64. What are the most evolved colors in the auric field?

65. What is the next most evolved?

66. What shades of colors should be avoided?

67. Is black always negative when it appears in the aura?

68. The shaman relies on "direct knowledge," as opposed to information accessible to the conscious mind. What is the difference? How is direct knowledge received?

69. Two of my former apprentices, who at my recommendation began studying with an Eastern master, told this story: One evening when everyone was sleeping, a cobra entered one of the bedrooms, crawled past six people sleeping on futons on the floor and bit a woman sleeping in the middle. Why do you think the cobra bypassed so many people, choosing to bite someone in the middle?

70. Our research has shown that a large percentage of people suffering from terrible relationships with a spouse or close family member were in catastrophic relationship with them in a previous life or lives. We personally have worked with some who have married their jailor, murderer or rapist. Can you think of two reasons for this madness to keep occurring?

71. What is nearly always needed, besides transmuting imprints, in the case of rape, assault, or physical or sexual abuse in childhood?

72. In this more informed age, how would you describe what is needed in soul retrieval?

73. Shamans capable of doing "retrieval" work by going into trance and "journeying" to the lower worlds are hard to find. What is an alternative and effective way for a practitioner to accomplish this very important task?

74. Once, while my thirteen-year-old daughter and I drove through the Blue Ridge Mountains, we began sharing animal stories. At one point I stated that we could make wild animals appear for us. Certain I was teasing her, she laughed and poked me (my daughter lived with her mother, my ex-wife, who did not share my beliefs). I decided to seize the opportunity to make my point, and so I said we would see a deer on the right side of the road when we got around the next curve. To her amazement, we did. How would you explain what happened since something beyond clairvoyance was involved? For

example, if I did see that deer with my inner vision, how do you explain the perfect timing for my discussion with my daughter?

75. What is meant by the statement that we are part of a "non-local" universe – something traditional shamans have always known?
76. On the basis of the above answer, how might distant healing work?

77. You are attempting to meditate in your home and work with spiritual practices, but there is a lot of traffic noise outside and a neighbor is using a weed eater. What should you do?

IV. Our Solutions to Thinking Outside the Box

1. Pull over. Find out where he got his "hooks" into you and use our procedure for removing them.

2. When entering a power spot, your body immediately lets go. This may cause temporary drowsiness. Avoid places where you feel energized, as they will drain you.

3. The aura of a community or land will open up to you. There will be a sense of flowing and acceptance by the land itself.

4. There will be a sense of foreboding or fear, or simply feeling restless and unsettled.

5. An ordinary event that for some peculiar reason grabs your attention is a sign. Also an extraordinary event is usually a sign.

6. The wilderness, outdoors and Nature are seen as a challenge, something to conquer. This idea creates separation from the ecstasy of merging with the natural world.

7. Not the angels or ascended masters or Michael. This is a job for "middle management," and the elementals are experts.

8. The drum, like the horse, takes you where you need to go. The rhythmic percussive beat will carry you into other levels with little effort on your part.

9. Become aware of fleeting images, nuances and subtle feelings that arise. Sense the shifts in energy, the boundaries you cross and the concentric rings. Above all, trust your first impressions and listen to your body.

10. The above are terms to describe the landscape of the energetic world, which is continually communicating vast amounts of information to you. It is just that your conscious mind needs training to access it.

11. Such a place connotes a complete "balance" of the directional forces. It forms a type of void within, which is the potential for all things.

12. Find a protected place in a clearing. Take off garments. Offer "smokes" to Wind devas and request this information. The winds may blow in several directions but only one will fill you. From what direction does it come?

13. There is more empowerment in becoming what you are *not* expressing than what you already *are* expressing.

14. From lack of meditation and similar spiritual practices, one gradually loses the integrity of what has been developed.

15. Information from the quantum universe is not accessed by focusing the mind as in the third dimension, but by indirect observation.

16. Because most of us have identified with the mind, which pulls the electrons of the Third Eye into the "particulate" state, where it becomes useless as a means of accessing the higher world. We have forgotten how to do what I call "indirect observation." It means that if we want to access information not available to the five senses or the conscious mind, we do not focus directly on it. We do not scrutinize. We observe and yet do not observe; we watch and do not watch at the same time. Remember: "attention" on the physical; "intention" on the transcendent. Otherwise, in our attempt to access information, we draw the Third Eye quantum particles into the physical, and lose the access to the higher plane.

17. The darkness just before dawn, because that phase is closest in vibration to the moment just before Creation, which I was blessed to experience in a powerful vision years ago.

18. Dusk! The crack between the outer and inner worlds.

19. Dawn to an hour after sunrise.

20. The midpoints (Feb. 2 Candlemas; May 1, May Day; Aug. 1, Lammas; Oct. 3, Sawain)

21. Dark of the moon. Less protection against "attack." There is an enlightened stage for every kingdom, meaning a species has completed its destiny in that category and cannot advance further without becoming something quite different.

22. (covered elsewhere)

23. Fragrances penetrate the veils between the planes and call the attention of other beings. They also cleanse us and our surroundings.

24. Meditation, non-doings, music, Nature, breath, art, being "present."

25. Fire, of course – it transmutes.
26. Air.

27. A cave.

28. Forest setting; large trees, rocks.

29. Water.

30. A contained space. A panorama of views can be distracting.

31. Lovingly accept them as part of your environment. Accept and embrace them. Your scent will change and they will lose interest. If you fight them, or get annoyed and irritated, your scent changes and they become aggressive. Try it! It takes a little practice but it works.

32. Listen to your body. Be attentive as well to subtle fleeting images.

33. Leave at once! Do not try to figure it out. Do not pass "go!" Do not collect $200.

34. If it grabbed your attention, it is a sign. If extraordinary, it is a sign.

35. The disciplines of the body and the disciplines of the mind are one and the same. Control of the body is control of the mind and vice-versa. Choose either or both.

36. Even without knowing what it is about, you can and should do a ceremony or prayer to change the energies, and the situation will be transformed and healed.

37. Usually "not me" indicates an attachment or a need for soul retrieval.

38. Lay them on the ground or floor in the fetal position and gently rock them, simulating the "womb." They will soon calm down.

39. Connect with the Wind elementals. Have them cease blowing, so the fire can burn itself out.

40. Through ceremony connect with the "entity" of the storm and intend it to be reduced to a tropical storm, or deflect it – but never to a populated area.

41. Round off the corners. The wall facing the client should be sky blue. All walls should be warm colors.

42. Use a de-possession ceremony. If it works, there is a possession. If it has no effect, then the client probably has a chemical imbalance.

43. Get a picture of the pet and visualize them returning.

44. You read with your body, not your mind.

45. Call in a great horned owl or coyote to frighten them away.

46. There is either spirit influence or an imprint has been activated.

47. When a person is in a coma, they are not in the physical body, but are usually wandering confused in their double. You would then

attempt to call the person back to the body; if you have the capability, go into trance, leave your body, find that person and bring them back.

48. When you are undergoing upheaval in your own life, or you are experiencing a loss of some kind, you never do medicine work (shamanic practices). You are too open and vulnerable. This is not the time for heroics. Your power is in honoring your healing process. Seek to connect your client or friend with another shaman. (You should always, for this reason, have colleagues you can call on, as they can call on you.)

49. If the proposed place is right, then the aura of the land and community will open up to you. There will be a palpable, bodily feeling of ease and quiet joy. Things will seem to flow. You seem to just meet the right people, and opportunities appear to open up.

50. The screaming, shrieking sound produces an orange/red. Every sound has a color correspondent. This shade of orange/red, when found in the aura, connotes "insanity." Can you imagine the effect of this sound on a person who has been in a major accident and is being rushed to the hospital? It can strike terror in their heart, especially if they are in a coma.

51. a) Disturbing dreams. b) It evokes feelings of sadness, depression, fear, anxiety, confusion or being drained.

52. a) The nature of the Bad Medicine; b) source; c) the element that is out of balance; d) is there a curse, the presence of wandering or bad spirits; e) is there an imprint from violence or tragedy in the past?

53. a) Are they human, elemental, demonic, extraterrestrial? b) What do they require?

54. These are beings of the Nature kingdoms that, like some humans, have lost their way. They feed off negative energy and can be quite destructive. They need to be returned with great compassion to their source, to Earth Mother.

55. By the nature of the energy there; for example, feelings of anger, violence and unnatural heat would connote negative or trapped Fire spirits. Calmness = water.

56. An "artificial elemental," one created by a dark magician, will simulate a negative elemental. They can be very dangerous! However, if you are in a state of balance, then you might choose to invite it to come into your energy field while you hold the idea that all energy is of the Creator and allow this energy to be healed by your loving acceptance. The result can be an ecstatic expression of light from the transmutation of that powerful but negative thought form. Be careful. You do not want to mistakenly draw in a living spirit which could cause problems.

57. These are the only languages whose vibrating patterns are in harmony with the patterns of the universe. There was a time in which many people could see into the etheric realms. They could see that the utterance of certain sounds set up certain etheric forms that would have different effects on one's consciousness. It is important, however, to get the pronunciation correct.

58. English is not a philosophical language. In the Greek New Testament, for example, there are five different words to express different types of love. In the English New Testament, there is but one word. Chinese, Tibetan, East Indian, Hebrew, Aramaic, Latin, Tibetan and Greek are philosophical languages and superior for communicating the higher truths to the "vulgar" and "romance" languages of Europe.

59. The power of the spoken word, of course. If you put sand on a plate of glass, you can observe how different sounds made with a musical instrument will create different patterns or designs in the sand. In a similar way, they affect our consciousness.

60. Calming = blues and violets; energizing = warms – red, orange, yellow; balancing = green.

61. Green can foster growth in a cancer tumor.

62. When there is irritation, anxiety, fear or inflammation.

63. Amethyst, Lapis and those of the blue-violet spectrum. This spectrum is incapable of carrying a negative charge.

64. The gem colors represent attributes that have reached perfection.

65. The pastels.

66. The cloudy or muddy colors.

67. No! Pure black represents hidden karmic work or a secret mission that cannot be gleaned by those of the negative path. Pure black is powerful. With off-black, however, it is a different story. A charcoal black can signify malice; blue-gray is depression.

68. The conscious mind uses a thinking process. "Direct knowledge" is gleaned directly through the Third Eye, the organ of higher consciousness, the second-hand intention.

69. Their teacher's explanation was that it was this person's unresolved negativity that attracted the cobra. I would agree, adding that the victim may have had a major imprint of abuse that had for some reason been activated. When an imprint is activated, it begins pulsating, sending out signals that have the effect of a negative magnetism.

70. Lack of forgiveness, hatred, blame, and harsh judgments bind us to that person and vice versa. The imprint of the experiences results in a negative magnetism that carries over into future lives in which we continue to attract each other, often for further pain and abuse. The "white magic" of forgiveness breaks the spell. But forgiveness must be verbalized with feeling, not repeated mechanically like ordering a pizza. The other reason is that a highly evolved soul would wish to help heal that abuser or persecutor of serious karma.

71. Soul retrieval.

72. Obviously the entire soul is not lost, but at the time of severe trauma a fragment of one's total consciousness can be split off and trapped in a time warp, so that the fragment keeps reliving the trauma along with the terror, etc., while the "self" experiences the growing feeling of something missing, lost or out of sync.

73. The practitioner guides the client to the moment of trauma, has her find the missing child, comforts the younger version, if necessary; informs the child of her connection and that she has come to take that child away from her pain; lovingly embraces her, and brings her forward to real time. A period of time may be needed to interact with her child in the days that follow.

74. There is no rational explanation. We live in a magical universe and a magical world that adapts itself to our needs. It was an opportunity for my daughter to begin thinking outside of the box, to step outside the conventional thinking that had been part of her life up to that time. I sensed that "portal of opportunity" and seized the moment. That deer had to be there!

75. The idea of distance between two planes is in connection with the illusion of the space-time continuum that we as a species accepted as a means of growth. Real separation does not exist.

76. In the seventeen-mile long Hadron Collider Particle Accelerator scientists have demonstrated that two photons, the tiniest known particles, are in total communication with each other to the point that one will travel at near light speed the exact same path as the other. One does not have to stretch to know that the same thing must be true with human beings. Scientists have theorized that, before the Big Bang, all matter in the universe was condensed to the size of a basketball. If this is the case, everything in the universe at that time was in contact with everything else.

77. Consider doing nothing, with the understanding that these distracting influences are part of the bio-diversity you chose in this lifetime. Instead of "fighting," try accepting it, and then spread out your extensive molecules, allowing it to flow through you without touching you. You will be amazed!

Other Works available by Peter Calhoun

Soul on Fire was released by Hay House Inc. on May 1, 2007 and is now available in bookstores nationwide.

Soul on Fire is a collection of true stories that describe the amazing spontaneous awakening of paranormal powers that accompanied Peter's spiritual journey.

You can preview Soul on Fire, and receive notices of future Peter Calhoun and other Hay House authors, by signing up through Peter's website at www.petercalhoun.com to download the introduction and four stories (in PDF Format).

NEW! Peter Calhoun Audio book - Soul on Fire

Now on Audio CD - Peter reading the complete text of Soul on Fire. Nine CDs with a tenth, bonus disc of MP3 files for the most portable listening experience. The cost is $25.00 + $4.00 shipping and handling (within US).

We are very pleased to offer this opportunity to hear the compelling stories of Soul on Fire, read by the author. You may order a copy through Paypal on petercalhoun.com or by mailing a check or money order for $29.00 to:

Cloudland Productions (Check or Money order Payable to Cloudland Productions)
Chuck Peters
7709 Old State Road
Cloudland, Georgia 30731

You can also get acquainted with Peter Calhoun on YouTube Video: "Mystery Us" program host, Tony Pratt, interviews Peter Calhoun at www.youtube.com.

Peter Calhoun on DVD

Walking Between the Worlds $30. In this 90-minute lecture, Peter discusses the unique time we are living in, how to release the energies of the old world and forge a new path as beings bearing our light into our New Millennium's new world, a coming Golden Age of Enlightenment.

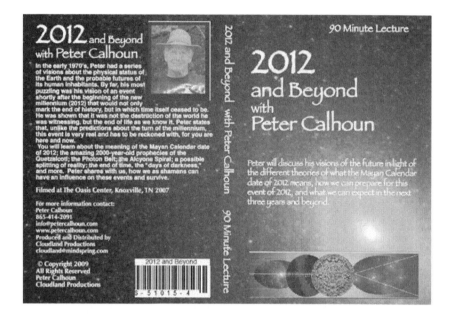

2012 and Beyond $30:   Peter discusses his early visions in relation to emerging events, and explains the different possible meanings of the 2012 Mayan Calendar date in relation to cosmic events involving the Alcyone Spiral, the "photon belt," and the coming "end of history," or end of life as we know it.

More Powerful Material from Peter Calhoun on DVD

Reincarnation, Karma and Destiny - A 3 hour workshop $55. Two DVD Set

In this packed 3 hour workshop, Peter brings to light many questions we have all had. Do we reincarnate and where have we been, what is karma and do I really have to pay back past life mistakes, and what is our Destiny, is it already written for us?

To See Without Eyes, To Hear Without Ears, To Know Without Thought- $20. A 45 minute Lecture

In this riveting lecture with an audience of over 500, the Coptics Conference in Johnson City was spellbound by Peter's sharing his experiences and insights of where we come from and who we really are.

Returning the Power to the People - $20. A 45 minute lecture
Speaking to a standing room only audience in Atlanta, Georgia, Peter shares his insights of what we have been told for hundreds of years just might not be the truth. What is the truth, who are we, and what we can do about coming into our own power are shared in this 45 minute lecture.

Healing, with Peter Calhoun $ 55. A 3 hour lecture
With the assistance of his partner, Astrid, Peter shares with everyone the true inherited gift of healing that we all possess. Peter and Astrid's Healing Techniques are shared and one becomes aware that we all have this ability.

TO ORDER:
You may order your copy of these materials via Paypal on petercalhoun.com or by mailing a check or money order for the stated amount plus an additional $4.00 shipping and handling cost for each DVD to:

Cloudland Productions (Check or Money order Payable to Cloudland Productions)
Chuck Peters
7709 Old State Road
Cloudland, Georgia 30731

Introducing Peter's newest works available in electronic format (E-books) and DVD's available at www.petercalhoun.com :

E-books by Peter can be downloaded from Peters' website www.PeterCalhoun.com, and purchased through Paypal.

Last Hope on Earth

A revolutionary approach to healing and wellness that can transform your life

In this newly released e-book, Peter and Astrid share the revolutionary healing technology that they have demonstrated in workshops throughout the US and Canada and which in private practice has enhanced the quality of life for hundreds of people.

The Association for Spiritual Ecology (ASE)

The ASE is a unique alliance between humans and the elemental kingdom that was requested of Peter and Astrid while hiking through the Smokey Mountain National Park. The alliance involves individuals and groups around the world conducting full moon ceremonies for healing our precious Earth. In these ceremonies, both global as well as local issues are addressed. For information see Peter's website at www.petercalhoun.com.

Apprenticeships, workshops and lectures

In addition to these outstanding publications, Peter offers apprenticeship programs and is available for lectures and workshops.

Peter and his talented partner, Astrid, are offering an ongoing International Apprenticeship Program which involves several four to six day apprenticeship gatherings for training in both the Eastern and Western US. The program includes instruction, ceremonial work and field trips into special natural areas to work with practices that will strengthen your connection to the Earth and the Nature kingdoms. For more information please call 865-414-2091 clearly stating your name and phone number if leaving a message, or see Peter's website at www.petercalhoun.com.

DEDICATION

This book is dedicated to all you brave souls who have the courage to break free of this prison without walls – our beloved Earth. You may not remember, but before you came into your present embodiment, you committed to demonstrate to many others how this was done by challenging the consensus reality – the agreed-on reality of the times – providing in your example a blazing testimonial of this eternal truth: that we are limited only by our beliefs about ourselves and our perception of the world.

Because of your great compassion for those trapped here by their ignorance and blind, unquestioning acceptance of the greatest deception in the history of our species, you elected to enter the waters of forgetfulness, knowing full well the risk involved of getting stuck in this veritable prison camp. You came here to spring the trap. You also were assured you would not be doing this alone – that there would be millions of others comprising a great Family of Light that would be joining you as a member of this vast extended family that came from many star systems, each with their own special wisdom and talent.

May each of you, and you know who you are by the resonance in your inner being, have the blessings of our Infinite Creator.

Made in the USA
Lexington, KY
19 September 2012